PROBLEM BOOK IN PHONOLOGY

CANADA INSTITUTE
OF LINGUISTICS

Bradford Books

Edward C. T. Walker, Editor. *Explorations in THE BIOLOGY OF LANGUAGE.* The M.I.T. Work Group in the Biology of Language: Noam Chomsky, Salvador Luria, *et alia.* 1979.

Daniel C. Dennett. *BRAINSTORMS: Philosophical Essays on Mind and Psychology.* 1979.

Charles E. Marks. *COMMISSUROTOMY, CONSCIOUSNESS AND UNITY OF MIND.* 1980.

John Haugeland, Editor. *MIND DESIGN.* 1981.

Fred I. Dretske. *KNOWLEDGE AND THE FLOW OF INFORMATION.* 1981.

Jerry A. Fodor. *REPRESENTATIONS: Philosophical Essays on the Foundations of Cognitive Science.* 1981.

Ned Block, Editor. *IMAGERY.* 1981.

Roger N. Shepard and Lynn A. Cooper. *MENTAL IMAGES AND THEIR TRANSFORMATIONS.* 1982.

John Macnamara. *NAMES FOR THINGS: A Study of Human Learning.* 1982.

Hubert L. Dreyfus, Editor, in Collaboration with Harrison Hall. *HUSSERL, INTENTIONALITY AND COGNITIVE SCIENCE.* 1982.

Natalie Abrams and Michael D. Buckner, Editors. *MEDICAL ETHICS: A Clinical Textbook and Reference for the Health Care Professions.* 1983.

Morris Halle and G. N. Clements. *PROBLEM BOOK IN PHONOLOGY: A Workbook for Introductory Courses in Linguistics and in Modern Phonology.* 1983.

PROBLEM BOOK IN PHONOLOGY:

A Workbook for Introductory Courses in Linguistics and in Modern Phonology

Morris Halle and G. N. Clements

A Bradford Book

The MIT Press
Cambridge, Massachusetts
and London, England

Seventh printing, 1994

Copyright © 1983 by
The Massachusetts Institute of Technology

This book is in a special program to extend the life of significant MIT Press titles. It has been produced using an on-demand printing process that allows the publisher to print books in relatively small quantities. Because of the nature of the process, printing quality may be slightly compromised in comparison to the original printing.

This book was set in Times Roman by Robert Ingria using the Xerox Dover laser printer with copy prepared by the SCRIBE text formatter running under Tops-20.

The cover was designed by Irene Elios.

ISBN 0-262-58059-4

Contents

Preface

In our teaching experience we have found that students get proper insight into the aims and methods of modern phonology only when they have had direct experience with attempts to grasp and express formally the principles and regularities inherent in a given body of data. Working out problems must, therefore, be an essential part of courses introducing students to modern phonology, whether the introduction is part of an introduction to linguistics or takes place in a separate course entirely devoted to phonology.

The workbook consists of an introductory essay and six chapters of problems. The introductory essay gives an overview of some of the principal results and assumptions of current phonological theory. It includes discussions of the phoneme, natural classes, distinctive features, phonological rules, and some recent developments in the treatment of prosodic phenomena.

Each of the six chapters of problems that follow is intended to provide "hands-on" experience with a major area of modern phonology. Chapter one, "Phonetics," provides some practice in transcription and the phonetic characterization of individual speech sounds. Chapter two, "Complementary Distribution," focuses on the presence of predictable information in the transcription and on ways in which it might be eliminated. Chapter three, "Natural Classes of Sounds," contains problems designed to introduce the student to the writing of formal rules. Its major focus is on the distinctive features and their functioning in phonological rules. Chapter four, "Phonological Rules," illustrates various considerations that are involved in the choice of the base form that best accounts for the alternations observed. Chapter five, "Rule Systems," concerns rule interactions, abbreviatory conventions, and rule ordering. In Chapter six, "Prosodic Phonology," are gathered a number of problems in the area of tone and stress, which are best dealt with by the devices of autosegmental and metrical phonology.

The problems have been used by the authors in their introductory courses, primarily at MIT and Harvard. They are meant to be used in conjunction with a textbook and/or other materials provided by the classroom instructor. The problems are taken from over 30 languages from all parts of the world and illustrate a wide variety of language types. Many are drawn from the authors' first-hand research; others have been taken from sources indicated at the end of the book. In all cases an attempt has been made to design the problems in such a way that they yield valid insights into the structure and analysis of the language from which they are drawn by including all relevant (and excluding all irrelevant) information.

The problems themselves contain a minimal amount of commentary and advice on how to go about finding a solution. We feel that in this way the set of exercises will be most readily adaptable to the different needs and viewpoints of each instructor and her/his students. Nor have we included in the book solutions to any of the problems, for it is our belief that much of the instructiveness of a good workbook lies in the opportunities it offers for comparing and evaluating alternative solutions for a given body of data, rather than in directing the student's attention to the "best" solution.

Morris Halle
G. N. Clements

Acknowledgments

We wish to express our gratitude to our students, who have helped us to improve these problems by their questions, answers, and other comments. We also thank our colleagues V. Bergvall, B. Joseph, S. Kuno, W. Poser, E. Sezer, and H. Thráinsson, who have generously contributed problems to this collection. Special thanks to Robert Ingria, who did the major type-setting work, and to Diana Archangeli and Brent Vine for proofreading and valuable comments on the text.

The sources of the different problems and information about the languages from which they were taken are given at the end of the book.

PROBLEM BOOK IN PHONOLOGY

Introduction

1. The Linguistic Basis of Phonetics

To those who have not thought much about it, the human ability to produce and perceive speech may not seem particularly remarkable. Indeed, we speak our native language with little conscious effort and are normally unaware of the chain of events that must be set into motion when we engage in a conversation with another speaker of our language. It is only when we begin to try to understand in detail how this everyday human activity is possible that we begin to appreciate its complexity. Phonetics is the study of one aspect of human language: its physical realization. It is concerned, then, with the way in which speech is produced by the vocal mechanism (articulatory phonetics), the physical properties of the speech sounds produced (acoustic phonetics), and the way in which these sounds are perceived by the listener (psychoacoustics).

In studying speech sounds, the first thing to observe is that we are not studying physical events as such. Rather we are dealing with certain events—physiological, acoustic, psychological—just to the extent that we judge them to involve human speech. We are concerned, as phoneticians, not with sounds pure and simple, but with sounds produced and perceived by particular organisms (human beings) who have access to a certain type of knowledge, which we term "knowledge of language." It is for this reason that not all noises produced by human beings are of equal interest to the phonetician. For example, the "ah" we are asked to produce when the doctor examines our throat or the noise we make in blowing out a candle are of little phonetic interest, even though speech sounds which are physically identical to these may happen to occur in language.

The best way to convince ourselves of the central role played by linguistic knowledge in the production and perception of speech is to consider the way we perceive spoken words. Our reaction to a speech event depends crucially on our linguistic experience. If we, as speakers of English, hear another English speaker produce the sequence of sounds that the phonetician symbolizes as [ˈpʰæs ðəˈ ʃugər], we will not "hear" these sounds as such but will "hear" the three word sequence *pass the sugar*. And yet there is nothing in the speech event itself that signals the end of one word and the beginning of another. It is only by virtue of our knowledge of English that we are able to "parse" this sequence of noises into recognizable English words. When the identical acoustic signal is presented to someone who has no knowledge of English, he can neither identify the words nor even tell us how many words are contained in the utterance.

The perception of intelligible speech is thus determined only in part by the physical signal that strikes our ears. Of equal significance to perception is the contribution made by the perceiver's knowledge of the language in which the utterance is framed. Acts of perception that heavily depend on active contributions from the perceiver's mind are often described as illusions, and the perception of intelligible speech seems to us to qualify for this description. A central problem of phonetics and phonology is then to provide a scientific characterization of this illusion which is at the heart of all human existence.

Since knowledge of a language is crucial for the perception and production of speech, it is natural to inquire into the character of this knowledge. Because of the central role that is played by the knowledge of words, it might be thought that our knowledge of a language consists of nothing more than a memorized list of words. That this can't be the case, that our knowledge of a language goes much beyond a memorized list of words, is shown by the following simple considerations. In (1) below we have given a small list of pseudo-words:

(1)   sprash, sdrut, strup, skrig, sflick, sblish, sknap, splim

If a group of English speakers were asked to rank these words on a scale ranging from those which could easily be adopted into English to those which most certainly could not, it is very likely that *sprash, strup, skrig,* and *splim* would rank high, while *sdrut, sflick, sblish,* and *sknap* would rank low. These responses on the part of English speakers show that our knowledge of the language cannot be limited to knowledge of a list of words. Since the pseudo-words in (1) were made up expressly for this "experiment," our subjects could not have memorized them. Their judgments must, therefore, be based on something else than a memorized list of words. We get some insight into the nature of this "something else" when we notice that the difference between the pseudo-words that are judged to be like English and those judged to be unlike English consists in the consonant sequences with which the words begin. Specifically, speakers judge that [spr, str, skr, spl, skw, sky] are admissible onsets of English words on the basis of their familiarity with words like the following:

(2)   spring   string   scrimp   splint   squint   skew

On the other hand, clusters such as [sdr, sbl, skn] etc. are inadmissible onsets in English words.

It is, of course, not plausible to suggest that when we were taught English we were made to memorize the list of all admissible onsets of English words. None of our subjects is likely to recall any childhood experience of this sort, nor are many parents likely to recall discussing with their children what consonant sequences may or may not begin English words. But from the fact that we have not been taught explicitly the list of admissible onsets of English, we may not conclude that we have also not learned them. Although teachers do not like to dwell on it for obvious reasons, there can be little doubt that most of what any normal person knows she or he has learned without being taught, and this is especially true with regard to knowledge of language, as any course in linguistics ought to make amply clear.

Having granted that some, or even most, of our knowledge of language is acquired without benefit of teaching, we still must explain why we learn the list of word onsets in the course of memorizing the words of the language. Is there any reason for us to focus on these onset lists rather than on a myriad of other facts like the last digit of the telephone number of our five best friends, or the middle initial of American Nobel Prize winners?

The only plausible answer that has ever been suggested is that our memory is so constructed that when we memorize words, we automatically also abstract their structural regularities. We suppose, to be specific, that human storage space for memorizing words is at a premium so that every word must be memorized in a maximally economical form in which redundant (predictable) properties are eliminated. Since the principles governing word-initial consonant clusters in English capture an important redundant property of English words, access to these principles allows speakers to store English words in their maximally economical, redundancy-free form. If we know that three-consonant onsets of English words all begin with [s], we do not need to store in our memory, when learning words such as those in (2), the information that allows us to distinguish [s] from all other consonants of the language. Since we can make this saving in memory storage for every word that begins with these consonants, it is to our obvious advantage to memorize the rule rather than to clutter up our memory with these redundant facts.

Different rules, of course, govern the words of different languages, but there is no language that lacks such principles altogether, that does not place severe constraints on permissible sequences of consonants and vowels in words. Hence it is always to the language learner's advantage to abstract the structural principles determining the shapes of the words because that allows him to store in a maximally efficient way the enormous vocabulary, amounting to many thousands of items, which all normal speakers carry in their heads.

The preceding remarks have an important implication for the form in which we must assume words are stored in our memory. The uninitiated observer might suppose, as a first hypothesis, that storage is in terms of unique acoustic images or Gestalts associated with each individual word, or perhaps in terms of certain habitual patterns of motor activity representing our pronunciation of each word. In this view, learning the sound shape of a given English word would be analogous to the way we learn the sound of the waves on the ocean or the movements involved in tying our shoelaces or putting on an overcoat. This form of memory, however, is incompatible with the results of the pseudo-word experiment described above. The results of that experiment imply that a crucial step in learning the words of a language consists of abstracting the principles that govern the permissible sequences of consonants and vowels in our language. If we memorized words as acoustic images or patterns of motor activity, it is totally mysterious how we could ever develop these principles. This mystery would be cleared up at once if we assumed that we perceive words unlike other physical events, that we perceive them not as acoustic images or as patterns of motor activity but as sequences of discrete speech sounds or *phonemes*.

It might be objected at this point that this claim entails the implausible presupposition that every normal human has a view of language that is identical with that of a person who has command of an alphabetic writing system, for there are obviously millions of perfectly normal speakers of ordinary human languages who are illiterate or who are literate in nonalphabetic writing systems. This objection fails to take into account the fact that we possess knowledge of a great many things without being consciously aware of it. One of the major pursuits of Socrates in Plato's dialogues was to make his interlocutors conscious of the huge body of knowledge that they possessed without being remotely aware of this fact. Whatever else one may think of Plato, he surely succeeded in establishing the existence of unconscious knowledge. In order to write in an alphabetic writing system, an individual must have conscious access to the phoneme sequences by means of which the words have been stored in his memory. The fact that all languages can be written in an alphabetic writing system shows that speakers of all languages can be made aware of this aspect of their linguistic knowledge. It does not mean that speakers must be consciously aware of this aspect of their knowledge in order to understand others or to speak themselves. It only means that we may possess knowledge without being aware of this fact. Indeed one may think of linguistics as the science that attempts to characterize in detail one type of such knowledge, namely that possessed by normal speakers of their mother tongue.

2. Distinctive Features

We have just seen that an essential component of the unconscious knowledge that speakers have of their mother tongue is constituted by representations of words as sequences of discrete phonemes. An important further discovery that has been made about the phonemes is that these are not further indivisible units, but are themselves complexes of attributes or features which recur in all human languages. We turn now, therefore, to an examination of the evidence that supports this view of phonemes as bundles of distinctive features.

The most obvious observation one might make about the process of speaking is that it involves a complicated set of maneuvers using the lips, tongue, and other structures at the upper end of our respiratory and digestive tracts. The production of natural speech requires the precise coordination of these various components in such a way as to attain a series of well-defined articulatory states or target configurations following upon each other in close succession in time. In order to see how these states are achieved, it is necessary to examine the activity of the components one by one.

When we speak, air comes from our lungs and excites the cavities in our nose, mouth, and throat, causing them to vibrate. When the cavities are excited in this way, they emit an audible sound. The nature of the sound that emerges is determined primarily by two factors: the precise manner in which the air in the cavities is excited, and the internal geometry of the cavity itself.

It is very easy to separate the contribution of these two components because we can readily keep one constant and vary the other. For example, when we sing or pronounce the vowel [a] on various pitches, we keep the geometry of our nose, mouth, and throat cavities constant, as we can verify by looking at a mirror. What changes in producing these various pitches is the way we excite these cavities. One way of exciting them in speaking is by forcing a rapid succession of little puffs of air through the vocal cords at the bottom end of our vocal tract. The mechanism by which we do this is quite similar to the mechanism by which we force air rapidly through our lips in order to express the fact that we feel cold. Although we cannot directly see the operation of the vocal cords as the air is forced through them, we can feel its effect by placing our fingers over the Adam's apple as we pronounce the words *I sigh* or *so-so*; we will then feel a slight tingle in our fingers as we pronounce the vowels, but none as we pronounce the consonants. The tingle indicates that English vowels are produced with vocal cord excitation, while its absence in the consonant [s] shows that the vocal cords are at rest in this consonant. Sounds produced with vocal cord vibrations are called *voiced*; sounds produced without vocal cord vibrations are called *voiceless*.

Returning now to the different pitches of the vowel [a], it can be shown that as the rate of the puffs of air passing through the vocal cords increases, the pitch of the vowel goes up, while as the rate decreases, the pitch goes down. Note, however, that as long as we keep the cavity geometry the same we go on producing the same vowel.

It is also possible to keep the manner of excitation constant and vary the cavity geometry. In this case, we produce a sequence of different vowels, all on the same pitch. This can once again be verified by watching the rapid movements of the jaw and lips in a mirror as we pronounce the vowels [i,e,a,o,u] in succession.

We have seen here that in producing a simple speech sound we must control at least two independent factors: the way we excite the cavity and the shape that we choose to give it. It is obvious that these two factors are quite unconnected. The excitation is controlled by the expansion and contraction of the lungs and by various adjustments that we make at the vocal cords. The geometry of the cavity, on the other hand, is controlled by the muscles that move the tongue, the lips, and other structures near them. This *componential* structure of speech sounds is their most striking property.

In addition to vocal cord excitation, there are two other types of excitation in speech. The first of these is turbulence or fricative noise produced by forcing air through a narrow constriction, as for example in producing the initial consonants in *so*, *foe*, and *show*. The second is called plosion and is produced by a sudden switching off and on of the air stream as in the medial consonants of *appear*, *attack*, and *acute*. It is easy to see that fricative noise and plosion are mutually exclusive types of excitation. Since fricative noise is produced only when air flows through the mouth, it is incompatible with plosion, which requires the flow of air to be totally interrupted. By contrast, both fricative noise and plosion can be produced either with or without vocal cord vibration. We thus have another example of the composite character of speech sounds: both fricatives and plosives appear in two varieties, one produced with vocal cord vibrations and the other without:

(3)

	fricatives	plosives
voiced:	v z ž	b d g
voiceless:	f s š	p t k

(Here [ž] indicates the last sound in *rouge* and [š] the first sound in *shoe*.)

The composite structure of speech sounds is not limited to the way we set an air stream into motion but extends equally to the way we control the geometry of our vocal tract. Consider, for example, the way we produce the final consonants in the words: *rub, Rudd, rug; rum, run, rung.* The configuration of the tongue, lips, and larynx is exactly the same for each of the pairs *rub* and *rum*, *Rudd* and *run*, and *rug* and *rung*. The only difference between the members of these pairs is that in producing the last sound of the second set of words (*rum, run, rung*), we lower the velum—the mobile wall visible at the back of the mouth when we say "ah," which terminates in the fleshy appendage known as the uvula—so that air from the lungs passes behind it and on up through the nose. This maneuver has the effect of exciting the air in the nasal cavity, a fact that we can quickly establish by placing a finger on the side of the nose while saying these words and prolonging the final sound: in doing so we discover a kind of vibration at the end of each of the words of the second set, but none at the end of the words of the first set. Sounds produced with a lowered velum are called *nasal*; those produced with a raised velum are *nonnasal* or oral.

As ordinary speakers we have no need, of course, to place a finger on the nose of the person with whom we are speaking in order to determine whether or not his nasal cavities are excited, for the obvious reason that when the nasal cavity is excited the acoustic output is modified in a specific way that our auditory system can readily detect. In much the same way we can determine whether or not someone's vocal cords are vibrating while producing a given sound without putting our fingers on the speaker's throat. Our auditory system is so constructed that it tells us whether a sound is voiced or voiceless. The same is also true of the other types of excitation, fricative noise and plosion; their presence or absence in a sound is readily perceived by our auditory system. Thus, the machinery we have for producing speech and for perceiving it operate in tandem. Both the muscles controlling the vocal tract, and the auditory system that analyzes the signal, treat speech sounds not as atomic, further unanalyzable entities but as simultaneous complexes of properties or features. Moreover, to a significant degree the set of properties in the two domains—articulation and perception—overlap. This close match between articulation and perception is quite surprising, for the two systems subserve radically different vital functions. The articulatory muscles are part of the alimentary and respiratory systems which functionally are quite unrelated to the auditory system.

We can easily go further with the decomposition of speech sounds. Consider, for example, the final sounds of the words of the following three sets:

(4) a.   lip, rub, leaf, leave, rim

  b.   lit, lid, tooth, lathe, rice, rise, wren, rich, ridge, rush, rouge

  c.   back, bag

The final sounds of the first set, which we may symbolize as [p,b,f,v,m], respectively, are produced with a constriction that is formed by the lower lip. We call these sounds *labial*. The final sounds of the second set, symbolized by [t,d,θ,ð,s,z,n,č,ǰ,š,ž], are produced with a constriction formed by raising the blade (extreme front) of the tongue. These sounds are called *coronal*. The final sounds of the third set, symbolized by [k,g], are produced with a constriction formed by raising the body of the tongue. Additional sounds produced with this part of the tongue include the final sounds of *bang*, symbolized by [ŋ], and of the German name *Bach*, symbolized by [x]. These sounds are termed *high* or *velar*.

Furthermore, for the purposes of the present discussion, we must identify the property of *stridency* as illustrated below:

(5)   strident sounds: [f,v,s,z,š,ž]

  nonstrident sounds: [θ,ð,x]

As will be noticed, strident sounds are produced by directing the airstream against a secondary obstruction—either the sharp edges of the upper teeth, as in the case of [f,v,s,z], or the alveolar ridge (the hard structure in which the upper teeth are embedded), as in the case of [š,ž].

The last property to be considered here is that which distinguishes the initial consonants in the words in (6a) from those in (6b):

(6) a.   mat   nat   let   rat   wet   yet

    b.   bat   tat   get   cat   vet   fat

In producing the set of initial consonants in (6b), the vocal tract is narrowed or totally closed so that air is trapped inside of it and, as a result, the air pressure inside the cavity is greater than that outside. By contrast, when the sounds in (6a) are produced, there is no obstruction to the air flow and no pressure build-up inside the cavity. It is customary to refer to the sounds in (6a) as *sonorants* and to those in (6b) as *nonsonorants* or *obstruents*.

We conclude this section with a list of distinctive features (7). This set of features is sufficient to define and distinguish, one from another, the great majority of the speech sounds used in the languages of the world. Many of the features on this list have been discussed above, but are included here for reference.

(7)   The Articulatory Correlates of the Distinctive Features

1. **syllabic/nonsyllabic:** [±syl]. Syllabic sounds are those that constitute syllable peaks, nonsyllabic sounds are those that do not. Syllabic sounds are typically more prominent than contiguous nonsyllabic sounds. (Vowels, syllabic consonants vs. glides, nonsyllabic consonants.)

2. **consonantal/nonconsonantal:** [±cons]. Consonantal sounds are produced with a sustained vocal tract constriction at least equal to that required in the production of fricatives; nonconsonantal sounds are produced without such a constriction. (Obstruents, nasals, liquids vs. vowels and glides.)

3. **sonorant/obstruent:** [±son]. Sonorant sounds are produced with a vocal tract configuration sufficiently open that the air pressure inside and outside the mouth is approximately equal. Obstruent sounds are produced with a vocal tract constriction sufficient to increase the air pressure inside the mouth significantly over that of the ambient air. (Vowels, glides, liquids, nasals vs. stops and fricatives.)

4. **coronal/noncoronal:** [±cor]. Coronal sounds are produced by raising the tongue blade toward the teeth or the hard palate; noncoronal sounds are produced without such a gesture. (Dentals, alveolars, palato-alveolars, palatals vs. labials, velars, uvulars, pharyngeals.)

5. **anterior/posterior:** [±ant]. Anterior sounds are produced with a primary constriction at or in front of the alveolar ridge, while posterior sounds are produced with a primary constriction behind the alveolar ridge. (Labials, dentals, alveolars vs. palato-alveolars, palatals, velars, uvulars, pharyngeals.)

6. **labial/nonlabial:** [±lab]. As the term implies, labial sounds are formed with a constriction at the lips, while nonlabial sounds are formed without such a constriction. (Labial consonants, rounded vowels vs. all other sounds.)

7. **distributed/nondistributed:** [±distr]. Distributed sounds are produced with a constriction that extends for a considerable distance along the midsaggital axis of the oral tract; nondistributed sounds are produced with a constriction that extends for only a short distance in this direction. (Sounds produced with the blade or front of the tongue vs. sounds produced with the tip of the tongue. This feature may also distinguish bilabial sounds from labiodental sounds.)

8. **high/nonhigh:** [±high]. High sounds are produced by raising the body of the tongue toward the palate; nonhigh sounds are produced without such a gesture. (Palatals, velars, palatalized and velarized consonants, high vowels and glides vs. all other sounds.)

9. **back/nonback:** [±back]. Back sounds are produced with the tongue body relatively retracted; nonback or front sounds are produced with the tongue body relatively advanced. (Velars, uvulars, pharyngeals, velarized and pharyngealized consonants, central vowels and glides, back vowels and glides vs. all others.)

10. **low/nonlow:** [±low]. Low sounds are produced by drawing the body of the tongue down away from the roof of the mouth; nonlow sounds are produced without such a gesture. (Pharyngeal and pharyngealized consonants, low vowels vs. all others.)

11. **rounded/unrounded:** [±round]. Rounded sounds are produced with protrusion of the lips; unrounded sounds are produced without such protrusion. (Rounded consonants and vowels vs. unrounded consonants and vowels.)

12. **continuant/stop:** [±cont]. Continuants are formed with a vocal tract configuration allowing the airstream to flow through the midsaggital region of the oral tract; stops are produced with a sustained occlusion in this region. (Vowels, glides, *r*-sounds, fricatives vs. nasal and oral stops, laterals.)

13. **lateral/central:** [±lat]. Lateral sounds, the most familiar of which is [l], are produced with the tongue placed in such a way as to prevent the airstream from flowing outward through the center of the mouth, while allowing it to pass over one or both sides of the tongue; central sounds do not involve such a constriction. (Lateral sonorants, fricatives and affricates vs. all other sounds.)

14. **nasal/oral:** [±nas]. Nasal sounds are produced by lowering the velum and allowing the air to pass outward through the nose; oral sounds are produced with the velum raised to prevent the passage of air through the nose. (Nasal stops, nasalized consonants, vowels and glides vs. all other sounds.)

15. **advanced/unadvanced tongue root:** [±ATR]. As its name implies, this feature is implemented by drawing the root of the tongue forward, enlarging the pharyngeal cavity and often raising the tongue body as well; [−ATR] sounds do not involve this gesture. ([+ATR] vowels such as [i,u,e,o] vs. [−ATR] vowels such as [ɪ,ʊ,ɛ,ʌ,a].)

16. **tense/lax:** [±tense]. Tense vowels are produced with a tongue body or tongue root configuration involving a greater degree of constriction than that found in their lax counterparts; this greater degree of constriction is frequently accompanied by greater length. (Tense vowels vs. lax vowels.) We note that this feature and the last (ATR) are not known to cooccur distinctively in any language and may be variant implementations of a single feature category.

17. **strident/nonstrident:** [±strid]. Strident sounds are produced with a complex constriction forcing the airstream to strike two surfaces, producing high-intensity fricative noise; nonstrident sounds are produced without such a constriction. (Sibilants, labiodentals, uvulars vs. all other sounds.) The feature [+strid] is found only in fricatives and affricates.

18. **spread/nonspread glottis:** [±spread]. Spread or aspirated sounds are produced with the vocal cords drawn apart, producing a nonperiodic (noise) component in the acoustic signal; nonspread

or unaspirated sounds are produced without this gesture. (Aspirated consonants, breathy voiced or murmured consonants, voiceless vowels and glides vs. all others.)

19. **constricted/nonconstricted glottis: [±constr].** Constricted or glottalized sounds are produced with the vocal cords drawn together, preventing normal vocal cord vibration; nonconstricted (nonglottalized) sounds are produced without such a gesture. (Ejectives, implosives, glottalized or laryngealized consonants, vowels and glides vs. all others.)

20. **voiced/voiceless: [±voiced].** Voiced sounds are produced with a laryngeal configuration permitting periodic vibration of the vocal cords; voiceless sounds lack such periodic vibration. (Voiced vs. voiceless consonants.)

3. Natural Classes of Sounds

In (2) we gave examples of the admissible three-consonant onsets in English words, and we argued at length that English speakers have knowledge of the admissible onsets of their language. We have as yet not stated the principle governing these onsets by virtue of which speakers can distinguish "possible" from "impossible" pseudo-words in a list such as (1). As a first approximation we may say that English words are subject to the limitation that in a three-consonant onset cluster, C_1 must be [s], C_2 must be one of the set [p,t,k], and C_3 must be one of the set [r,l,w,y].

An important aspect of this limitation is that it involves not just random sets of phonemes but sets that share some features in common. Thus, for example, the set [p,t,k] shares the features [− voiced, − continuant], whereas the set [r,l,w,y] shares the features [+sonorant, − nasal]. And we find shared features in all sorts of phonological regularities in all sorts of languages: they generally involve natural classes of phonemes.

To cite one other example where the set of sounds [p,t,k] plays a role in English phonology, we observe that these sounds are pronounced with a special puff of breath or aspiration when they occur word-initially before stress as, for example, in such words as *pill, till, kill*. When these phonemes occur in other environments, they are not aspirated, as, for example, in *spill, still, skill*. In order to see more clearly what is involved in these cases, it is useful to examine the natural classes of phonemes as defined in the feature list (7). Let us assume, as proposed by Roman Jakobson, that phonemes are nothing but bundles or complexes of features and that therefore the only way that we can refer to a phoneme is by listing the features that compose it. When we attempt to follow this procedure, we discover that we need not list for each phoneme all features given in (7), but rather a smaller set of "defining" features. Thus, for example, we may uniquely designate the phoneme [p] by the four features:

(8) [− sonorant, +labial, − voiced, − continuant]

It is not possible to omit any of these features, for if we did we would be identifying not a single sound but a set of sounds. For example, if we omitted the specification of the feature [continuant], we would be identifying the set [p,f]; if we omitted the specification of [voiced], we would identify the set [p,b], and if we omitted the specification of [labial], we would identify the set [p,t,k], i.e., the set that can occupy the middle position in English three-consonant onsets and also is subject to aspiration word initially before stress.

Unlike the sets just reviewed, a set like [p,r] can be identified only by specifying more features than are required for each of the two sounds individually. In order to identify the set [p,r], we would have to specify the disjunction (9):

8

(9) [− sonorant, + labial, − voiced, − continuant]

or

[+ sonorant, − labial, − nasal, + coronal, − high, + continuant]

which mentions all the distinctive features required to identify [p] and [r] separately. We can now define the difference between "natural" and "unnatural" classes of sounds in the following way: "natural" classes can be specified by a single conjunction of features as in (8); "unnatural" classes require a disjunction for their specification as in (9).

We have already noted that the languages of the world appear overwhelmingly to favor natural sets of sounds in their rules. Translated in terms of feature specifications of the sort just illustrated, this means that the languages of the world prefer to deal with sets of sounds that require few specified features for their identification rather than sets that require many. If we now postulate that the rules and regularities that represent a speaker's knowledge of the phonology of his language are represented in the speaker's memory in terms of distinctive feature specifications, then this observed preference on the part of the languages of the world becomes readily comprehensible: it is but another facet of the need to conserve space in the speaker's memory, which we have already had occasion to invoke in accounting for the results of our "experiment" with the pseudo-words in (1).

4. Phonological Rules and their Interactions

Phonology—as opposed to phonetics—is not primarily concerned with the physical or sensory properties of speech sounds as such, but with the systems of rules that determine their possibilities of combination and their phonetic realization in each language. Students of language have long realized that the sounds of language are governed by rules of various sorts. Some of the greatest achievements in 19th century linguistics, for example, involved the discovery of the effects of such phonological rules or "sound laws" on the course of historical change. Thus, for example, part 1 of Grimm's Law replaces [p,t,k] by [f,θ,x], respectively, while part 2 replaces [b,d,g] by [p,t,k]. However, although the discovery of sound laws was extensively pursued by linguists for well over a century, little attention was paid to the exact nature and psychological status of these laws.

Largely as a result of work carried out since the end of the Second World War, it has become clear that a central component of every speaker's knowledge of language consists of rules of grammar, including phonological rules. As already noted, such rules are not directly accessible to conscious reflection; and most of us become aware of them only under very special circumstances. For example, one of the common difficulties that we encounter in speaking a foreign language is to remember to suppress the phonological rules of our native language. Thus, English-speaking tourists in France will normally betray their origins unmistakably in their pronunciation of words like *Paris* by their non-French aspiration of the initial sound (following, inappropriately in this case, the English aspiration rule), and their insistence on pronouncing the English retroflex [ɹ] instead of the (French) uvular [r] for the medial sound.

As a further example of a phonological rule of English consider the following pairs of words:

(10) seating   seeding

writing   riding

beating   beading

coating   coding

9

The majority of speakers of American English, in normal conversational speech, pronounce the words of the first column identically to the words of the second column, producing the orthographic *t* and *d* as a lightly articulated, voiced sound formed with a constriction produced by the tongue tip that we will symbolize as [D] ("tap"). What is interesting is that these words are not pronounced identically if the ending *-ing* is removed: *seat* is distinct from *seed*, *write* is distinct from *ride*, and so forth. We are clearly dealing here with a further rule of English phonology, which causes the phonemes [t] and [d] after a stressed vowel to be realized as a tap whenever another vowel follows in the same word.

This rule of English is particularly instructive, for two reasons. The first is that it shows us that underlying distinctions between phonemes can be merged or neutralized by the operation of regular phonological rules. As a consequence it is not always possible to determine the underlying (phonemic) representation of a word on the basis of its surface (phonetic) representation, for in dialects where *riding* and *writing* are pronounced indistinguishably, it will not be possible to decide for any given utterance of these words whether the last stem consonant is underlyingly [d] or [t].

The second point derives from the observation that not all dialects completely suppress the difference between words with underlying [t], such as *seating*, and words with underlying [d], such as *seeding*. An important phonetic difference between *seat* and *seed* lies in the fact that the vowel of the second word is produced with perceptibly greater length than that of the first. This is due to a regular rule of English according to which a vowel has greater duration before a voiced consonant than before a voiceless consonant. Further examples of this rule include *lap* versus *lab*, *lock* vs. *log*, *bus* vs. *buzz*. For the speakers of the dialect in question, this length distinction is preserved in the words *seating* and *seeding*, even though the difference between the orthographic *t* and *d* has itself been completely neutralized.

The reader who normally uses the tap sound in words like *seating/seeding* may easily ascertain whether he or she belongs to this latter dialect group by performing the following test. Write down the words *seating* and *seeding* on a sheet of paper, in random order with ten examples of each. Ask an English-speaking acquaintance who shares your dialect as nearly as possible to serve as subject. Read the list word by word to your subject, leaving enough time between each word so that the subject can write down the word she or he hears. If you make a consistent difference in length between the vowels of *seating* and *seeding* (and if, moreover, your subject has detected this difference), the subject's test score should be close to 100% correct. If, however, you do not make a distinction (or if your subject has not noticed your distinction), the expected score will be about 50% correct (the result that could be obtained by random guessing.)

How may we account for the difference between speakers of the dialect that maintains a vowel length distinction between *seating* and *seeding* (let us call this dialect A) and speakers of the dialect which preserves no difference between these words (let us call this dialect B)? We know that both dialects share the two phonological rules in question: the tap rule, and the rule which lengthens stressed vowels before voiced consonants. The difference between the dialects must, therefore, be attributed to the way the two rules interact. Whereas in dialect A the rules interact so as to maintain the two forms as phonetically distinct, in dialect B the same two rules interact so as to eliminate the phonetic contrast.

This difference in rule interaction can be captured formally if it is assumed that the rules of the phonology are applied in a specific order, that when a rule applies to a word it modifies the representation of the word, and that the rule ordered *n*th in the sequence of rules applies not to the underlying representation of the word, but rather to the representation created by the rule ordered before it. This type of computation of the surface form or phonetic output has been called a *derivation*. In (11) we illustrate the derivations of the words *seating* and *seeding* in the two dialects A and B. Notice that in dialect A the lengthening rule is ordered before the tap rule, while in dialect B the tap rule is ordered before the lengthening rule (vowel length is indicated by a colon).

(11)

Dialect A

	seating	seeding
Lengthening rule	—	i:
Tap rule	D	D
Output	s[iyD]ing	s[i:yD]ing

Dialect B

	seating	seeding
Tap rule	D	D
Lengthening rule	i:	i:
Output	s[i:yD]ing	s[i:yD]ing

The principle of rule ordering makes it possible to account for a great variety of fascinating phonological phenomena in terms of the interaction of a few simple rules. Rule ordering is, therefore, extensively represented in the problems collected in this book.

5. The Nature of Phonological Representations

We have so far tacitly assumed that phonological representations have the form of linear concatenations of phonemes, in much the same sense that written English consists of concatenations of letters. Notice, however, that written English does not provide a fully adequate analogy for phonological representation, since there is much information of relevance to spoken English that is not preserved in the standard writing system. One such type of information is stress. For example, when the word *convert* is used as a verb, main stress falls on the second syllable (*they will convert to the metrical system*), but when this word is used as a noun, main stress falls on the first syllable (*he is a convert to the metrical system*). This distinction is maintained even when these words are pronounced out of context.

A further aspect of English that is systematically omitted in the linear representations of written language is intonation: the "melody" with which a word, phrase, or sentence is pronounced. For example, if we produce the sentence *the Red Sox lost again* with a "flat" intonation, falling at the end, this sentence is understood as a statement of fact. If, on the other hand, this sentence is produced with a rise in pitch at the end, it is understood as a question, or if the rise is very great, as an expression of incredulity. Nearly all known languages make systematic use of stress and intonation in giving phonetic form to their sentences. Of special interest in this connection are the so-called tone languages where differences in pitch are used to distinguish one word from another. In the Ewe language of Africa, for example, [to] spoken with a high pitch may mean either "mountain" or "ear"; spoken with a rising pitch, it means "mortar," and with a low pitch, "buffalo." To represent such properties of language, writing systems have traditionally been supplemented with a set of diacritic marks. Thus, the Ewe words just discussed are commonly represented in studies of this language as shown in (12):

(12)   tó 'mountain', 'ear';   tŏ 'mortar';   tò 'buffalo'

It is possible to think of representations such as those in (12) in two distinct ways. On the one hand, one may view the diacritic marks as a means of extending the letter stock of our alphabet. From this point of view the difference between the symbols *ò* and *ó* is parallel to that between *o* and *e* or *m* and *n*. Alternatively, it is possible to view the diacritic tone marks as representing phonetic entities that are separate but equal to those represented by the consonant and vowel letters. The appropriate analog here is the musical score of a song for a single voice unaccompanied. In the score, the text is represented by a sequence of letters, and the melody by a sequence of notes, the two sequences of symbols running in parallel on two separate lines or tiers.

For reasons to be detailed below, we adopt the latter view. Following Goldsmith (1979), we propose that the Ewe words will be represented as in (13), where tones and phonemes are represented on separate *autosegmental* tiers and where association lines link the tones to the phonemes that "bear" or manifest them:

(13) phoneme tier: to   to   to
                             | ∧ |
      tonal tier: H   LH   L

If tones are represented as a sequence of units on a tier separate and equal to that of the phonemes, then it is not necessary that the units on one tier should coincide one:one with units on the other tier. The fact that the autosegmental notation permits a one:many relationship between units on two tiers is a strong point in its favor, for it is this relationship that we find in actual languages. As illustrated in the second example of (13), a given vowel may be pronounced with an entire sequence of tones or melody. Moreover, a given tone may be held over any number of vowels or fractions of vowels, as we shall now see.

In the Ngizim language, verbs in the perfective are characterized by the tone melody LH, whereas in the subjunctive, verbs have the melody L if they begin with a syllable of the shape Cə, and the melody H otherwise. The following examples illustrate:

(14) perfective: jà kə̀ rú   'we stole'

                       jà kàasú   'we swept'

      subjunctive: jà kə̀ rì   'that we steal'

                       jà káaší   'that we sweep'

In this language, we see that verb tenses are characterized by different tone melodies, depending in part on the character of the first syllable. Using our multitiered notation, we may represent these forms as follows:

(15)   k ə ru   kaa su   k ə ri   kaa ši
        | | | | V   V
        L H   L H   L   H

We observe that the subjunctive morpheme, consisting of a single H tone or a single L tone, might be regarded as "discontinuous" in the sense that it is realized on discontinuous or nonadjacent parts of the word.

Tone is not the only phonological feature that may appear on a separate tier. Other features that characterize domains smaller or larger than a single segment may also be treated in this way. Indeed, in many languages we find strong evidence that the "skeleton" or canonic shape of a word should be abstracted as an entity distinct from the particular consonants or vowels that characterize it. The evidence in these cases is much the same as that which led us to recognize tonal "melodies" in languages like Ngizim.

Let us consider an example from Semitic, drawn from McCarthy (1981). In most Semitic languages, words are commonly formed from triliteral roots consisting of three consonants, such as [ktb] which has the general notional meaning 'write'. This root serves as the basis for constructing words according to strict canonic patterns. Thus, for example, in Classical Arabic verb roots, the canonic shape CVVCVC is associated with the grammatical meaning 'reciprocal' while the canonic shape CVCCVC is associated with the grammatical meaning 'causative'. Aspect and mood are determined by vowel "melodies" consisting of one to several vowels which extend across the word much as do the tones of Ngizim. Any verb in Classical Arabic, then, can be analyzed into three simultaneous components: the consonantal root, the CV-skeleton, and the vowel melody. From the root [ktb] we can form the following stems, among others:

(16) CVVCVC: kaatab 'correspond' (perfective active)

                   kuutib 'correspond' (perfective passive)

      CVCCVC: kattab 'cause to write' (perfective active)

                   kuttib 'cause to write' (perfective passive)

We see that the C-positions in the CV-skeleta are "filled" by the consonants of the particular root (here, the root [ktb]), while the V-positions are occupied by the vowels of the vowel melody, [a] in the case of the perfective active, [ui] in the case of the perfective passive. What emerges from these examples is that whenever there are more C-positions than consonants, or more V-positions than vowels, one of the consonants or vowels "spreads" to occupy the extra position. This is apparent in representations like the following, where each morpheme is assigned to its own tier:

(17)

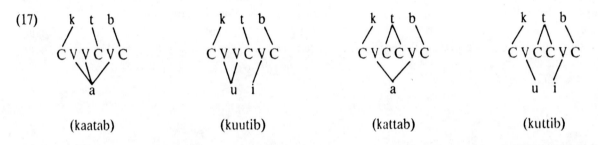

    (kaatab)   (kuutib)   (kattab)   (kuttib)

We see in the case of the perfective active forms that a single vowel may spread over nonadjacent positions in the CV-skeleton, just as in Ngizim a L or H tone melody spreads to all vowels within the word. That the same is true of consonants can be seen most strikingly in the case of roots having only two consonants in their melody, such as [sm] with the general meaning 'poison'. For this root, the verb stems that correspond to those given above for 'write' are *saamam*, *suumim*, *sammam*, and *summim*, respectively. In these words we see that the second consonant of the root melody spreads over all noninitial positions of the CV-tier:

(18)

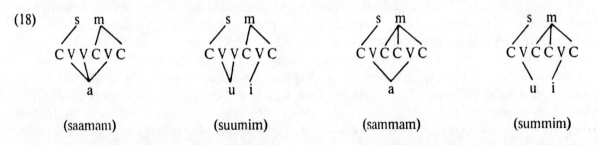

    (saamam)   (suumim)   (sammam)   (summim)

The CV-skeleton, which plays a morphological role in Semitic languages, may play a phonological role in others, accounting for such properties as length, syllabicity, and timing even when these are not associated with specific grammatical meanings (see Clements and Keyser (1981 and forthcoming)). Consider, as an example, the following nouns in Turkish:

(19)

	nom	dat.	'his'	'our'
'room'	oda	odaya	odası	odamız
'stalk'	sap	sapa	sapı	sapımız
'mountain'	da:	daa	daı	daımız
'la' (note)	la:	la:ya	la:sı	la:mız

These forms illustrate various suffixes used in the nominal inflection. We see from examining the first and second examples that the suffixes [-ya] and [-sı] are used after nouns ending in vowels, while [-a] and [-ı] are used after nouns ending in consonants. Similarly, the choice between [-mız] and [-ımız] depends upon whether the noun ends in a vowel or a consonant in the uninflected form. The third and fourth examples illustrate the fact that there are two kinds of long vowels in Turkish: those that (like the long vowel of *da:*) pattern like consonants in noun inflection, and those that (like the long vowel of *la:*) pattern like vowels. Notice that this patterning is perfectly regular: if a final long vowel patterns like a consonant in one inflected form, it patterns like a consonant in all other inflected forms.

These differences can easily be accounted for if we make two assumptions: first, that length is represented in Turkish just as it is in Arabic, by the association of a single phoneme with two adjacent positions on the CV-skeleton, and second, that a long vowel may be associated with either of the sequences VV or VC. Given these assumptions, we may represent the crucial difference between 'mountain' and 'la' in the following way:

(20)
```
    C V C        C V V
    |  V         |  V
    d  a         l  a
```

From these representations it is evident that the rules accounting for the correct form of suffixes need only be sensitive to whether a noun stem ends in a C or a V on the CV-tier.

We see, then, that consonants and vowels, like tones, may "spread" over more than one position in a word. This parallelism between tones, on the one hand, and consonants and vowels, on the other, naturally raises the question of whether more than one nontonal feature may be linked with a single element of the CV-skeleton, just as more than one tone may be linked to a single vowel (see (13) above). In fact, there is good reason to suppose that this is the case. As many phoneticians have pointed out, the initial sounds of English words like *chip* and *job* consist of two components: a stop followed by a fricative, each of which is similar to phonemes that occur independently in English (compare the initial sound of *chip* with the initial sounds of *trip* and *ship*). Nevertheless, we cannot consider these sounds to consist simply of the two independent phonemes [t] and [š], since elsewhere in English no word may begin with a sequence consisting of a stop followed by a fricative (*tšip, ksip, dzip*). One way of expressing the fact that these sounds behave as single phonemes with regard to the distributional rules of English even though they are phonetically complex is to represent the feature "continuant," which distinguishes stops from fricatives, on a separate tier. Given this assumption, the words *ship* and *chip* differ only in respect to their representation on the continuant-tier, not on the remaining tiers:

(21)
```
continuant-tier:    +c +c −c        −c +c +c −c
                    |  |  |          V  |  |
CV-tier:            C  V  C          C  V  C
                    |  |  |          |  |  |
other features:     Š  I  P          Š  I  P
```

(here we use lower-case *c* on the top tier to represent the feature "continuant" and upper case letters on the bottom tier to represent bundles of features not including the feature "continuant"). Other types of complex segments found in the world's languages, such as prenasalized stops, appear to be susceptible to this type of treatment as well.

6. The Constituents of the Word

In the preceding section, we have developed the view that a phonological representation is a three-dimensional object, whose core is constituted by the C and V slots of the skeleton around which are disposed tiers consisting of distinctive feature bundles (consonants and vowels) which are linked to different slots in the skeleton. A full phonological representation may thus consist of a CV core surrounded by several autosegmental tiers containing information about such features as tone, nasality, point of articulation, and glottal states; i.e., about the phonetic properties of the C and V slots of the core.

The three-dimensional character of phonological representations makes it possible to solve another long-standing problem, in this case involving the fact that words are organized simultaneously into sequences of morphemes, on the one hand, and sequences of syllables, on the other. Until quite recently linguists assumed that the only way of delimiting sequences within the word was by means of junctures or boundary markers of various kinds. One problem with this device is that it introduces all sorts of additional symbols into the representation that, if taken seriously, make the statement of phonological rules very cumbersome. This problem is illustrated in (22), where "+" represents boundaries between morphemes and "/" represents boundaries between syllables:

(22) $+/\text{in}+/\text{ter}+/\text{ment}+/$ $\qquad$ $+/\text{o}/\text{ri}/\text{gi}/\text{n}+\text{a}/\text{l}+\text{i}/\text{ty}+/$

In the word *interment*, as this representation shows, syllable boundaries and morpheme boundaries coincide, while in *originality* the syllable organization is quite unrelated to the morpheme organization. The opacity of these representations is a direct consequence of the fact that they are assumed to consist of feature complexes and juncture marks strung together in a single line. Once we view phonological representations as three-dimensional objects, as explained above, we have at our disposal a much more perspicuous way of dealing with the problem. Instead of delimiting the constituents by means of boundary symbols, we can represent each of the constituents on a separate tier as shown below (σ = syllable, μ = morpheme).

(23)

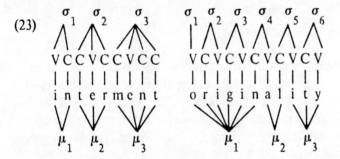

7. Metrical Structure

All languages have restrictions on what phonemes can combine into sequences, and, as we have seen, speakers can readily tell whether or not a given sequence of phonemes would constitute a well-formed word in their language. As many linguists have noted, the domain over which a great many such constraints hold is the syllable. We have already discussed an example of this. By a rule of English, word-initial consonant clusters consisting of three members must have the form [s]+[p,t,k]+[l,r,w,y]. That this rule is in fact a constraint over syllables rather than over words is shown by the fact that it accounts for word-internal constraints on consonant sequences as well. Thus, while well-formed, existing words like *construct* and *astronomy* can be broken up into sequences of well-formed syllables (con-struct, a-stro-no-my), ill-formed "pseudo-words" like *consknuct* and *apftonomy* cannot. The phonological deviance of the latter can be explained in terms of this fact. Many other rules of English phonology can be shown to involve the syllable in their statement as well.

In addition to rules such as the one just illustrated, which involves restrictions on possible sequences of phonemes within the syllable, there are many rules that are sensitive to distinctions in what has been called *syllable weight*. Syllables that end in a single short vowel are termed *light syllables* and all other syllables are termed *heavy syllables*. We have already seen an example of a language in which syllable weight plays a phonological role: Ngizim. Many other languages are sensitive to this distinction as well. In this section we shall be concerned with examining an important class of rules which are frequently found to be sensitive to syllable weight: stress rules.

In languages making use of stress as a phonological property, each word is characterized by the fact that one syllable is singled out as the bearer of main stress. In the simplest case, this syllable is completely predictable, coinciding with a fixed position in the word counting from the beginning or end. Thus, for example, in Czech or Latvian main stress falls on the first syllable of the word, in Swahili main stress falls on the penultimate syllable, and in Turkish or Farsi main stress falls on the final syllable.

In other languages stress placement, while predictable, is subject to further principles which determine patterns of alternating stress across the word. In Maranungku, main stress falls on the initial syllable, and secondary stress falls on every second syllable thereafter. In Weri, main stress falls on the final syllable, with secondary stress falling on every second syllable before it. Examples are given below:

(24) Maranungku: lángkaràtetì   'prawn'   wélepènemànta   'kind of duck'

      Weri: àkunètepál   'times'   uÌùamít   'mist'

A third factor that frequently enters into the determination of stress placement is, as mentioned above, syllable weight. A simple case is represented by Latin. In this language, main stress fell on the penultimate syllable, if this syllable was heavy, and otherwise on the antepenultimate:

(25) Latin: magíster   'teacher'   tábula   'board'

                legú:men   'vegetable'   aurícula   'ear'

The variety of stress systems that we have reviewed so far can be viewed as resulting from a small number of simple rule types which recur in one language after another in slightly different forms. For example, we have seen that there are rules that assign main stress to one end of the word or the other (Czech, Swahili, Turkish); rules that assign secondary stress in an alternating pattern from a fixed starting point (Maranungku, Weri); and rules that assign stress to heavy syllables only (Latin penultimate stress). More complex systems can be described as involving combinations of these rule types.

We shall here offer an informal account of the theory of stress that has come to be developed under the name of *metrical phonology*. While our account will be kept informal, our basic principles can be translated into the formal framework of metrical phonology in a straightforward way. The reader desiring a fuller account of this approach is directed to the work by Liberman, Prince, Hayes, Halle and Vergnaud, and others listed in the references at the end of this introduction.

It will be assumed that the theory of phonology recognizes two distinct ways of concatenating syllables (and other entities, as we shall see directly) into a sequence. One of these is the familiar joining together of entities like beads on a string, where the only relevant property is the position of one unit relative to the others. The second means of concatenating entities consists of setting up one unit as the *head* governing either its immediate neighbor or the entire substring of units on its right or on its left. Graphically we may picture this type of concatenation by means of *trees* such as those illustrated in (26), where the σ's on the bottom row represent the individual syllables in the sequence.

(26)

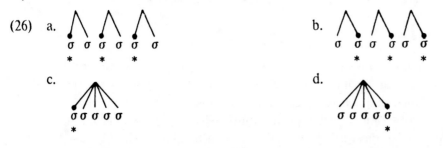

We have indicated the fact that a syllable is a head by **dotting** the branch of the tree dominating it. In the trees in (26a) the head governs its immediate neighbor on the right, while in (26b) the head governs the immediate neighbor on the left. Such trees will be called *bounded*. They contrast with the *unbounded* trees in (26c,d), where the head governs the entire sequence of units on its right in (26c), and on its left in (26d).

We shall assume that aligned with each sequence of syllables is a *metrical grid* which is composed of a sequence of slots, one slot for each syllable in the string. A slot may be empty or filled by an asterisk in accordance with the convention (27).

(27)   Place an asterisk in the grid slot of a head.

The metrical grid permits us to read off the stresses on the different syllables of the word by the simple expedient of equating degree of stress with the number of asterisks aligned with a particular syllable. This convention accounts for the placement of asterisks in (26) and below.

The diagram in (26c) will be taken here as the formal way of representing stress contours of the words in a language like Czech or Latvian, where each word has only a single stress, which is located on the first syllable. Similarly, the diagram (26d) represents stress in a language like Turkish or Farsi, where the final syllable is the only stressed syllable in the word. Stress assignment in a language like Czech or Latvian will therefore be stated as in (28):

(28)   a. Over the syllables of the word, construct a left-headed unbounded tree.

        b. Construct the corresponding metrical grid, placing asterisks in conformity with (27).

Notice that (28b) is not an independent rule of the language but the automatic consequence of the decision to represent the stress contours of words by means of metrical grids. The rule for stress assignment in a language with word final stress will be identical to (28), except that the tree will be right-headed rather than left-headed.

We now inquire as to how the proposed framework would express the stress rules of Swahili, where stress falls on the penultimate syllable. The stress contours of Swahili words thus resemble those of Turkish or Farsi, except that the final syllable is systematically left out of consideration. To account for this type of stress system, which is quite common, we make use of the diacritic mark *extrametricality*, which can be assigned only to syllables that are final or initial in the word and which has the property (29):

(29)   An extrametrical entity is excluded from metrical trees.

We can now state the stress rules of Swahili as in (30):

(30)   a.   The word final syllable is extrametrical.

        b.   Over the syllables of the word, construct a right-headed unbounded tree.

        c.   (28b)

The trees and grids in (26a) and (26b) represent words with stress on odd-numbered, respectively even-numbered syllables. Alternating stress contours of this type are found in such languages as Maranungku and Weri. They fail, however, to express the fact that two degrees of stress are distinguished in the words of these languages and that the initial, respectively final syllable of the word has greater stress than the rest. We capture this type of stress subordination by constructing a second layer of metrical trees whose bottom termini are not the syllables but the roots of the trees in (26a,b) as shown in (31):

(31)   a.   b.

In other words for languages such as Maranungku and Weri we need stress rules such as those in (32) and (33) respectively.

(32)   a.   Over the syllables of the word, construct left-headed bounded trees.

        b.   Over the roots of the trees in (a), construct a left-headed unbounded tree.

(33)   a.   Over the syllables of the word, construct right-headed bounded trees.

        b.   Over the roots of the trees in (a), construct a right-headed unbounded tree.

Notice that in conformity with (27) we have placed an additional asterisk in the grid slot corresponding to the head of each new tree.

It turns out that not only may languages distinguish between primary and secondary stress, as do Maranungku and Weri, but that some languages (for example, English; see below) distinguish three levels of stress. This fact is correlated with yet another fact, namely that in the languages of the world there are at most three layers of trees in the metrical structure of words, named respectively from bottom to top: *foot*-layer, *cola*-layer, *word*-layer. To reflect this formally, we shall assume that metrical grids always consist of three rows of slots. If there is only one layer of tree structure, the asterisks are inserted in the word-layer row; if there are two layers of structure, asterisks are placed in the foot-layer and word-layer row, as illustrated in (34) with respect to the trees in (31):

(34) a.   b.

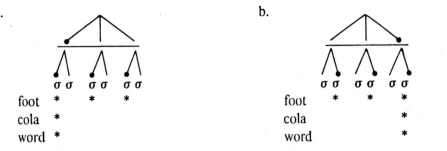

```
foot   *    *    *          foot   *    *    *
cola   *                    cola             *
word   *                    word             *
```

In (34) an asterisk has been placed in the cola row in spite of the fact that in the tree diagram there are only two layers of structure. In the light of (27) a "hole" in the grid should have been expected in the cola row. To fill this "hole" we invoke the special convention (35):

(35) If an asterisk is placed in a particular slot in the metrical grid, the slot on each "inferior" row is automatically filled with an asterisk. [The foot row is "inferior" to the cola row which in turn is "inferior" to the word row.]

We have so far reviewed stress systems of several relatively simple types and seen how they are to be treated within our formal framework. More complex systems can be described in terms of the interaction of the principles developed above. Consider, for example, a stress system which combines the tree construction rules of (33) with the extrametricality rule of Swahili (30a). Such a system would place main stress on the penult syllable and secondary stress on alternating syllables preceding the penult. This situation is exemplified in Warao, as shown by words like the following:

(36)   yàpurùkitànehàse 'verily to climb'   enàhoròahàkutái 'the one who caused him to eat'

We derive these patterns by means of the constructions in (37) where the extrametrical syllable is enclosed in parentheses:

(37) a.   b.

            yapurukitaneha(se)   enahoroahakuta(i)

```
            *   *   *   *                      *   *   *   *
                        *                                  *
                        *                                  *
```

The assignment of stress by means of bounded (binary) feet to a string consisting of an even number of syllables is completely straightforward (see (37b) above). However, when such trees are to be constructed over a string containing an odd number of syllables, a question may arise as to how to deal with the extra odd syllable. Specifically, we may ask whether or not the extra syllable is to be treated as the head of a (single-branch) tree. The fact that in (37a) the initial syllable bears stress, shows that languages treat such leftover syllables as heads.

This fact has further consequences of some interest. Up to this point, in our examples left-headed bounded trees were constructed from left to right, and right-headed bounded trees were constructed from right to left. Notice, however, that left-headed bounded trees can also be constructed from right to left, or right-headed trees from left to right. As the example in (38) shows, different kinds of stress contours will emerge depending on the end of the word from which tree construction begins:

(38) a. left to right tree construction:

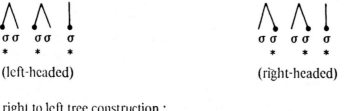

(left-headed)   (right-headed)

b. right to left tree construction :

(left-headed)   (right-headed)

We see, thus, that direction of tree construction may differentiate stress patterns of words. The question is, then, whether this option is available to natural languages.

An answer to this question is provided by a comparison of the stress contours of words in Maranungku (see (34a)) in which trees are constructed from left to right, with the stress contours of words in Garawa, in which trees must be constructed from right to left. Thus, we find Garawa examples like those in (39) which illustrate the principles in (40):

(39)
    1
    punjala   'white'

    1   2
    watjimpaŋu   'armpit'

    1   3   3   2
    nařiŋinmukunjinamiřa   'at your own many'

(40) a. Primary stress falls on the initial syllable.

    b. Secondary stress falls on the penultimate syllable.

    c. Tertiary stress falls on alternating syllables preceding the penultimate, except that

    d. There is no stress on the second syllable.

We account for these facts with the help of the rules in (41):

(41) a. Over the syllables of the word, construct bounded left-headed trees starting from the right end of the word.

    b. Over the roots of the trees of (a), construct a left-headed unbounded tree.

    c. Construct the corresponding metrical grid in conformity with convention (27).

In (42) we illustrate the effects of these rules on the examples quoted in (39):

20

(42)

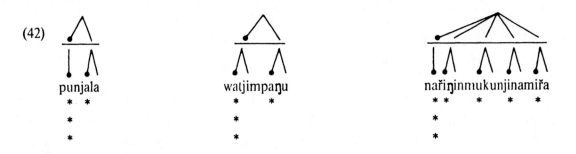

punjala   watjimpaŋu   narịŋinmukunjinamiřa

We note that the constructions in (42) fail to capture the facts in (40) in two respects. They do not indicate that the penultimate syllable has secondary rather than tertiary stress and they wrongly imply that there is stress on the second syllable. We cure these inadequacies by adding the two rules in (43), of which the first deletes an asterisk in position directly after primary stress, and the second enhances the stresses on the penultimate syllable from tertiary to secondary:

(43)   a.   Delete an asterisk in position directly after the primary stress.

        b.   Enhance the final foot-layer stress by adding an asterisk on the row directly below it.

These rules have the effect of changing (42) to (44), which represents the correct output (as the trees remain the same as in (42), they are omitted):

(44)   punjala   watjimpaŋu   narịŋinmukunjinamiřa

To summarize the discussion so far, we have seen that languages construct stress systems of great variety from an extremely small number of rule types. In particular, the following options in selecting rule systems have been identified:

(45)   a.   Extrametricality rule: present or absent.

        b.   Number of layers of tree construction: 1, 2, or 3.

        c.   Type of tree: bounded vs. unbounded; left-headed vs. right-headed.

        d.   Direction of tree construction (limited to bounded trees): left-to-right vs. right-to-left.

To conclude this discussion of metrical structure, we turn to an examination of the stress system of English. For reasons to become apparent below, we first consider stress in suffixed adjectives. As shown in the examples in (46), in adjectives formed with the suffix -ic primary stress falls on the presuffixal syllable:

(46)   Àsiátic   cryptogámic   mònotónic   phòtográphic

        Icelándic   sulphúric   climáctic   magnétic

        fanátic   generic   aquátic   dramátic

By contrast, as shown in (47), before the suffix -al primary stress falls on the presuffixal syllable only if it is heavy; if the presuffixal syllable is light, primary stress falls on the antepenultimate syllable:

21

(47)   sùpernátural   ànecdótal   àccidéntal

         binómial   primével   noctúrnal

         evéntual   cerébral   larýngeal

Notice that the stress distribution in (47) follows the same regularities as that of the Latin examples given earlier in (25). We shall assume with Hayes (1981) that the suffixes in the words above (and in adjectives in general) are extrametrical. We assume further that in addition to extrametricality, languages have at their disposal a second diacritic feature, the *accent*, which is used to mark the location of phonologically unpredictable stresses. This feature will be indicated here by underlining the accented syllable. Rules of accent placement apply before tree construction, and trees produced by these rules must incorporate accented syllables as heads. In the case of the English examples in (46) and (47) we shall assume that both suffixes, -*ic* and -*al*, are extrametrical but that they differ in the way they assign accent to their stems.

The suffix -*ic* is special in that it is one of a small number of suffixes that trigger a special rule of accent placement which we state in (48):

(48)   Assign accent to the last metrical syllable.

The suffix -*al*, on the other hand, represents the general case of stress in suffixed adjectives. Such adjectives undergo rule (49), which is identical to the Latin Stress Rule. In fact, there is evidence that this rule was incorporated into English as a consequence of the wholesale borrowing of words of Latin origin.

(49)   Assign accent to the last metrical syllable if it is heavy.

In addition to accent assignment and extrametricality, English word stress is the result of the tree and grid construction rules (50):

(50)   a.   Over the syllables of the word, construct left-headed bounded trees starting from the right end of the word.

       b.   Over the roots of the trees of (a), construct a right-headed unbounded tree.

       c.   Construct the corresponding metrical grid in conformity with conventions (27) and (35).

We illustrate application of (48--50) to examples with -*ic* below, where extrametrical syllables are parenthesized, and accented syllables are underlined:

(51)

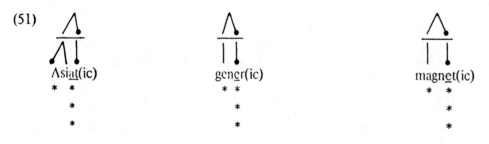

We note that since we are constructing left-headed trees from right to left and the right-most syllable (being accented) must be a head, the right-most foot will always be a nonbranching (degenerate) foot. If the word contains two or more syllables to the left of the accented syllable, the nonbranching foot will be preceded by a branching foot, as in *Asiatic*. If the word has only one additional syllable to the left the prefinal foot will be nonbranching, as in *generic* and *magnetic*.

The grids produced in (51) do not correspond precisely to the phonetic facts as given in dictionaries such as J.S. Kenyon and T.A. Knott, *A Pronouncing Dictionary of American English* (G.C. Merriam Co., Springfield, 1944). Kenyon and Knott distinguish four degrees of stress. For example, in normal pronunciations of words like *hermaphroditic* and *ambassadorial* we find primary stress on the penultimate, respectively antepenultimate syllable, secondary stress on the second syllable, tertiary stress on the first syllable, and no stress on the remaining two syllables. In the Kenyon and Knott system of transcription, primary stress is marked by placing a raised vertical stroke to the left of the syllable in question and secondary stress by a lowered vertical stroke to the left of the syllable. Syllables with tertiary stress are distinguished from those without stress by the presence of a full vowel as opposed to a reduced vowel (schwa [ə] or sometimes [ɪ]). Thus, for example, we find transcriptions such as the following, in which we have added subscript numbers to indicate the degree of stress:

(52) hermaphroditic

$$h\mathfrak{J}\underset{3}{,}\,mæfr\,ə\,\underset{2}{'}dɪt\underset{1}{ɪ}k$$

       ambassadorial

$$æm\underset{3}{,}\,bæs\,ə\,\underset{2}{'}dorɪ\underset{1}{ə}l$$

When we examine Kenyon and Knott's transcriptions of the three adjectives in (51), we find that the first syllable in *Asiatic* has a secondary stress, that in *generic* has a schwa, while *magnetic* is given with a full vowel without a stress mark (i.e., tertiary stress). Thus, our procedure yields the correct stress contour only in the last of the three words. To obtain the correct stress contours in the other two words, two supplementary rules are needed. First, noting that reduction affects only lax vowels that are unstressed, i.e., have no asterisk, we propose an asterisk deletion rule that is rather similar to the asterisk deletion rule of Garawa (43a):

(53) Delete an asterisk aligned with a light syllable in position directly before a stressed syllable.

Second, to obtain secondary stress on the first syllable of *Asiatic*, we require a stress enhancement rule resembling the rule proposed earlier for Garawa (43b):

(54) Enhance a foot-layer stress by adding an asterisk on the cola row if the next syllable has no asterisk.

These rules apply to the metrical grids in (51) to produce the following surface representations:

(55) 2 1   1   3 1
    Asi<u>at</u>(ic)   gen<u>er</u>(ic)   magn<u>et</u>(ic)
     * *   *   * *
     * *   *   *
       *   *   *

The stress contours of the adjectives in *-al* given in (47) are obtained in precisely the same fashion as those just discussed, except that these words do not trigger the special accent rule (48). Instead, accent is assigned to a heavy penultimate syllable by (49). Otherwise the general tree construction rules (50) apply. Stress deletion (53) and stress enhancement (54) function in exactly the same way as in the earlier examples. We illustrate this below:

(56)

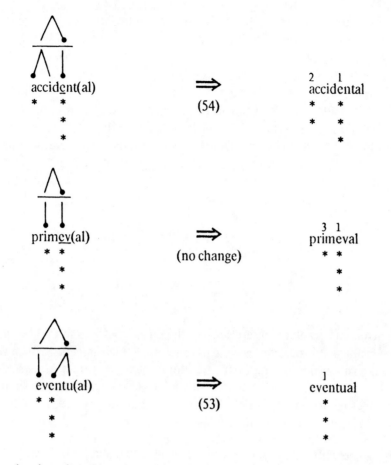

accident(al) ⇒ (54) accidental

primev(al) ⇒ (no change) primeval

eventu(al) ⇒ (53) eventual

The set of rules developed to this point, without further modification, assigns the correct stress contours to longer words in *-ic*, and *-al* as well, as shown below:

(57)

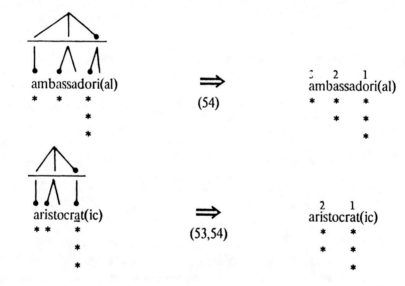

ambassadori(al) ⇒ (54) ambassadori(al)

aristocrat(ic) ⇒ (53,54) aristocrat(ic)

syncategoremat(ic)

$\Rightarrow$

(54)

3 2 2 1
syncategoremat(ic)

The rules developed to this point are not limited to stress assignment in adjectives but (excepting rule (48), which is triggered only by a small number of suffixes such as -*ic*) account for the regular pattern of stress assignment in English nouns. We illustrate this result with the following examples. In column A we have placed nouns whose penultimate syllable is light, in columns B and C nouns whose penultimate syllable is heavy. (Note that here as in most English nouns the final syllable is extrametrical.)

(58) A

B

C

America
1

Eliza
1

enigma
1

Andromeda
3   1

Pandora
3   1

hydrangea
3   1

incunabula
2   1

Gorgonzola
2   1

influenza
2   1

erotomania
2   1

Monongahela
2   1

extravaganza
2   1

intelligentsia
3 2   1

Ticonderoga
3 2   1

impedimenta
3   2   1

extrasyllabicity
2   2   1

onomatopoeia
2   2   1

counterpropaganda
2   2   1

25

Further Reading

Sections 1, 2, 3, 4:

Chomsky, Noam, and Morris Halle, *The Sound Pattern of English*, Harper and Row, N. Y., 1968.

Dell, François, *Generative Phonology*, Cambridge University Press, London, 1980.

Kenstowicz, Michael, and Charles Kisseberth, *Generative Phonology: Description and Theory*, Academic Press, N. Y., 1979.

Ladefoged, Peter, *A Course in Phonetics*, second edition, Harcourt Brace Jovanovich, N. Y., 1982.

Zue, Victor W., and M. Laferriere, "An Acoustic Study of Medial /T,D/ in American English," *Journal of the Acoustical Society of America* 66.4, 1039—50, 1979.

Sections 5, 6:

Clements, G. N., and S. J. Keyser, "A Three-tiered Theory of the Syllable," *Occasional Paper* no. 19, Center for Cognitive Science, M.I.T., 1981 (and *CV Phonology* forthcoming).

Goldsmith, John, *Autosegmental Phonology*, I.U.L.C and Garland Publishing, N.Y., 1979.

Halle, Morris, and Jean-Roger Vergnaud, "Three-Dimensional Phonology," *Journal of Linguistic Research* 1.1, 83—105, 1980 (and forthcoming).

Kahn, Daniel, *Syllable-based Generalizations in English Phonology*, I.U.L.C. and Garland Publishing, N.Y., 1980.

McCarthy, John, "A Prosodic Theory of Nonconcatenative Morphology," *Linguistic Inquiry* 12, 373—418, 1981.

Section 7:

Hayes, Bruce, *A Metrical Theory of Stress Rules*, I.U.L.C., 1981.

Halle, Morris, and Jean-Roger Vergnaud, *Three-Dimensional Phonology* (forthcoming).

Liberman, M. Y., and A. S. Prince, "On Stress and Linguistic Rhythm," *Linguistic Inquiry* 8, 249—336, 1977.

Prince, A. S., "Relating to the Grid," *Linguistic Inquiry* 14, 1983.

Selkirk, E. O., "The Role of Prosodic Contours in English Word Stress," *Linguistic Inquiry* 11, 563—605, 1980.

1. Phonetics

Transcription Key

Consonants

	Bilabial	Labio-dental	Inter-dental	Dental, Alveolar	Palato-alveolar	Palatal	Velar	Uvular	Pharyngeal	Glottal
Stop voiceless	p			t	č	c	k	q		ʔ
voiced	b			d	ǰ	ɟ	g	ɢ		
voiced implosive	ɓ			ɗ			g̢			
Fricative voiceless	ɸ	f	θ	s	š	ɕ	x	χ	ħ	
voiced	β	v	ð	z	ž	ʑ	γ	ʁ	ʕ	
Nasal (Stop)	m	ɱ		n	ň	ɲ	ŋ	N		
Lateral Approximant				l	ľ	ʎ				
Central Approximant				r		y	w			h

R-Sounds

In narrower transcription the following symbols can be used for r-sounds:

  ɾ or ř = alveolar tap   ɹ = alveolar approximant

  r̃ or r̃ = alveolar trill   ʀ = uvular trill

Other consonant symbols and diacritics

ʃ = š	C' = glottalized, ejective	C̣ = retroflex, emphatic
ʒ = ž	Cʰ = aspirated	C̥ = voiceless
j = y	Cʷ = rounded	C̩ = syllabic
ç = ɕ	Cʸ = palatalized	C̪ = dental
¢ = ts	C: = long	Ɇ = velarized, uvularized
υ = β	C̄ = tense, fortis	ⁿC = prenasalized

Vowels

	Unrounded				Rounded		
	Front	Central	Back		Front	Central	Back
	i	ɨ		HIGH	ü		u
	ɪ						ʊ
	e	3		MID	ö		o
	ɛ	ʌ			ɔ̈		ɔ
	æ	ɐ		LOW			
	a	ɑ					ɒ

Other vowel symbols and diacritics

y = ü	Ṽ = nasalized
ø = ö	V: = long
œ = ɔ̈	V́ = stressed
ɯ = ɨ	V̆ = extra-short
ɤ = 3	V̯ = nonsyllabic
ɩ = ɪ	ꞟ = centralized
ɷ = ʊ	V̥ = voiceless

The symbol ə (schwa) is often used to designate a mid central unrounded vowel of brief duration. ɝ , ɚ indicate retroflex central vowels.

Chart of Distinctive Features

1. Vowels: [+syl, −cons, +son]

	i	ɪ	ɨ	ü	u	ʊ	e	ə	ɛ	ɜ	ʌ	ö	ɔ̈	o	ɔ	æ	a	ɑ	ɒ
high	+	+	+	+	+	+	−	−	−	−	−	−	−	−	−	−	−	−	−
low	−	−	−	−	−	−	−	−	−	−	−	−	−	−	−	+	+	+	+
back	−	−	+	−	+	+	−	−	+	+	−	−	+	+	−	+	+	+	+
labial	−	−	−	+	+	+	−	−	−	−	−	+	+	+	+	−	−	−	+
tense	+	−	+	+	+	−	+	−	+	−	+	−	+	−				−	+

2. Sonorant consonants and glides: [−syl, +son]

	m	ɱ	n	ň	ɲ	ŋ	N	l	ĺ	ʎ	r	y	w	h	ʔ
cons	+	+	+	+	+	+	+	+	+	+	−	−	−	−	−
nas	+	+	+	+	+	+	−	−	−	−	−	−			
lat	−	−	−	−	−	−	−	+	+	+	−	−	−	−	
cont	−	−	−	−	−	−	−	−	−	−	+	+	+	+	−
cor	−	−	+	+	+	−	−	+	+	+	+	−			
lab	+	+	−	−	−	−	−	−	−	−	−	−	+		
ant	+	+	+	−	−	−	−	+	+	−	+	−	−		
spread	−	−	−	−	−	−	−	−	−	−	−	−	−	+	−
constr	−	−	−	−	−	−	−	−	−	−	−	−	−	−	+
high				+	+	−				+		+	+		
back				−	+	+				−		−	+		

3. Obstruents: [−syl, +cons, −son]

−voiced	p	p'	Φ	f	t	t'	θ	s	š	c	ɕ	k	k'	x	q	χ	ħ
+voiced	b	ɓ	β	v	d	ɗ	ð	z	ž	ɟ	ʑ	g	g'	ɣ	G	ʁ	ʕ
cont	−	−	+	+	−	−	+	+	+	−	+	−	−	+	−	+	+
cor	−	−	−	−	+	+	+	+	+	+	+	−	−	−	−	−	−
lab	+	+	+	+	−	−	−	−	−	−	−	−	−	−	−	−	−
ant	+	+	+	+	+	+	+	+	−	−	−	−	−	−	−	−	−
constr	−	+	−	−	−	+	−	−	−	−	−	−	+	−	−	−	−
high											+	+	+	+	−	−	−
back										−	−	+	+	+	+	+	+
low											−	−	−	−	−	−	+

Notes.

1. A blank entry indicates that the sound may be specified as either + or − for the corresponding feature.

2. Affricates such as /č, ǰ/ are treated as explained in the Introduction, page 14.

3. The feature *distributed* is not included on these charts. For discussion of this feature, see Introduction, page 6.

4. Palatalized consonants are produced with a high, front tongue position for which the feature characterization is [+high, −back].

5. Velarized consonants are produced with a retracted tongue position, and are thus characterized as [+back].

6. Retroflex consonants are produced by raising and retracting the tip of the tongue and are thus characterized as [+cor, −ant, −distr].

7. Aspirated consonants are characterized as [+spread].

Phonetic Transcription

1. Using the phonetic alphabet given above, transcribe the following English words as you pronounce them in casual speech. Do not base your transcription on overly slow, precise pronunciation, and be careful not to confuse the sounds of a word with its spelling.

1.	easy	17.	genuine
2.	judge	18.	through
3.	pack	19.	Italy
4.	optic	20.	how
5.	yellow	21.	filed
6.	coughs	22.	field
7.	teacher	23.	merry
8.	houses	24.	often
9.	bicycle	25.	orange
10.	Mary	26.	hoarse
11.	pastrami	27.	mountain
12.	whether	28.	valuable
13.	arise	29.	weather
14.	accept	30.	children
15.	marry	31.	doors
16.	horse	32.	look

2. The following broad transcriptions represent the normal pronunciation, in casual speech, of a speaker from Ohio. Write the word or words represented by each transcription, and indicate the differences (if any) between this dialect and your own pronunciation.

1.	[brɛθ]	13.	[plɛžər]
2.	[peyd]	14.	[taməs]
3.	[dɔg]	15.	[how]
4.	[θæŋk]	16.	[ɔt]
5.	[trɪk]	17.	[ayərn]
6.	[trawt]	18.	[wɪč]
7.	[amənz]	19.	[myuwl]
8.	[ǰaliy]	20.	[šæk]
9.	[ðɛm]	21.	[yuwz]
10.	[ənʌf]	22.	[saykaləǰiy]
11.	[kwiyn]	23.	[ɛkstrə]
12.	[pɔyzɪn]	24.	[ʔʌʔow]

37

Minimal Pairs

Illustrate the English phonemic contrasts given at the left with minimal pairs, one exhibiting the contrast in initial position and the other in final position, if possible. The first example is done for you.

		initial position	final position
1.	/p, b/	pie, buy	rope, robe
2.	/t, d/		
3.	/k, g/		
4.	/f, v/		
5.	/θ, ð/		
6.	/s, z/		
7.	/m, n/		
8.	/n, ŋ/		
9.	/r, l/		
10.	/č, ǰ/		
11.	/š, ž/		
12.	/p, f/		
13.	/d, z/		
14.	/t, θ/		
15.	/d, ð/		
16.	/š, č/		
17.	/h, w/		
18.	/s, θ/		

39

Phonetic Description

1. Give a phonetic description of the sounds that are represented by the following symbols. The description should mention (in order and where relevant) voicing, oral/nasal, point of articulation, manner of articulation (stop, fricative, etc.), and anything else of importance.

    a. [t]

    b. [v]

    c. [γ]

    d. [ɟ]

    e. [β]

    f. [k]

    g. [m]

    h. [ŋ]

    i. [pʰ]

    j. [ɓ]

    k. [t']

    l. [d̥]

    m. [ṣ]

    n. [e]

    o. [ɔ]

    p. [ay]

    q. [ɪ]

2. What is the phonetic symbol for the following sounds?

    a. a glottal stop

    b. a voiceless alveolar lateral

    c. a voiceless velar fricative

    d. a low front unrounded vowel

    e. a lower high back rounded vowel

    f. the sound you make when you blow out a candle

41

2. Complementary Distribution

Angas Sonorants

Voicing is predictable in Angas sonorants. State the rule.

1.	mut	'to die'	13.	fʷaṇ	'to rain'
2.	nuŋ̥	'to ripen'	14.	tam̥	'bench'
3.	ntaŋzum̥	'wasp'	15.	ŋgak	'snake'
4.	mbaŋga	'drum'	16.	ndarm̥	'bark'
5.	nemʸel̥	[name of village]	17.	pampam̥	'bread'
6.	sir̥	'to forgive'	18.	lɛp	'to send'
7.	liːliː	'slowly'	19.	dondoṇ	'yesterday'
8.	ʔara	'road?'	20.	ʔar̥	'road'
9.	kʷal̥	'joint'	21.	tarwep	'harvest season'
10.	kʷɔnsar̥	'finger'	22.	dɛŋ	'to drag'
11.	mɓɛlm̥	'to lick'	23.	potiŋ̥	'sky'
12.	nfʷarm̥	'head cold'	24.	zigɔl̥	'Satan'

Kongo Obstruents

In Southern Kongo, we find [t, s, z] in complementary distribution with [č, š, ž], respectively:

1.	tobola	'to bore a hole'	9.	nselele	'termite'
2.	čina	'to cut'	10.	lolonži	'to wash'
3.	kesoka	'to be cut'	11.	zevo	'then'
4.	nkoši	'lion'	12.	ažimola	'alms'
5.	zenga	'to cut'	13.	nzwetu	'our house'
6.	žima	'to stretch'	14.	kunezulu	'to heaven'
7.	kasu	'emaciation'	15.	tanu	'five'
8.	čiba	'banana'			

1. State the distribution of these sounds. Where do [t, s, z] occur? Where do [č, š, ž] occur?

2. Which sounds should be taken as representing the basic (underlying) phonemes, and which as representing their surface variants? State your reasons.

   basic:

   nonbasic:

3. State the rule that derives the surface variants from the basic phonemes you have proposed.

47

Ewe Liquids

1. In Ewe, [l] and [r] never occur in identical environments. It is possible to derive them from the same underlying phoneme. State the rule governing the distribution of [l] and [r] in terms of *classes* of phonemes.

   Note. [kp] and [gb] are labiovelar stops, that is, sounds articulated with simultaneous closure at the lips and velum.

1.	zrɔ̃	'to be smooth'		15.	dru	'to be bent'
2.	ɲra	'to rage'		16.	fle	'to pluck'
3.	lɔ̃	'to love'		17.	glamaa	'uneven'
4.	kpla	'to intertwine'		18.	litsa	'chameleon'
5.	mlagoo	'thick'		19.	dzre	'to quarrel'
6.	gblaa	'wide'		20.	ɣla	'to hide'
7.	lolo	'to be large'		21.	xloloo	'rough'
8.	wlu	'to dig'		22.	tsro	'bark (of tree)'
9.	βla	'suddenly'		23.	Φle	'to buy'
10.	srɔ̃	'wife'		24.	blema	'formerly'
11.	lãkle	'leopard'		25.	dɔlele	'illness'
12.	hle	'to spread out'		26.	ŋlɔ	'to write'
13.	vlɔ	'to go far away'		27.	yre	'evil'
14.	atra	'mangrove'		28.	adoglo	'lizard'

2. Notice that in loanwords, Ewe sometimes has [l] where the donor language has [r]:

1.	German	Krug	>	Ewe	kplu	'jug'
2.	French	Paris	>	Ewe	kpali	'Paris'
3.	Portuguese	claro	>	Ewe	klalo	'finished'
4.	Danish	trappe	>	Ewe	atrakpoe	'steps'

It is obviously not the case that Ewe speakers "cannot pronounce the sound *r*". How does the rule you stated above help to explain this apparently irregular behavior?

Ganda Liquids

1. [r] and [l] are in complementary distribution in one variety of Ganda. State the conditions under which each appears.

1.	kola	'do'	11.	wulira	'hear'
2.	lwana	'fight'	12.	beera	'help'
3.	buulira	'tell'	13.	jjukira	'remember'
4.	lya	'eat'	14.	eryato	'canoe'
5.	luula	'sit'	15.	omuliro	'fire'
6.	omugole	'bride'	16.	effirimbi	'whistle'
7.	lumonde	'sweet potato'	17.	emmeeri	'ship'
8.	eddwaliro	'hospital'	18.	eraddu	'lightning'
9.	oluganda	'Ganda language'	19.	wawaabira	'accuse'
10.	olulimi	'tongue'	20.	lagira	'command'

2. Consider the following loanwords (from English except for the last item). How may one account for the apparently aberrant treatment of [r] and [l]?

1.	ebendera	'flag'	3.	luula	'ruler'
2.	leerwe	'railway'	4.	ssaffaali	'safari' (from Swahili)

Papago Stops

In Papago, the dental stops [t, d] are in complementary distribution with the palato-alveolar stops [č, ǰ]. State the rule that accounts for their occurrence.

Note. [ĭ] is an extra-short vowel.

1.	bíǰim	'turn around'	10.	hɨwgid	'smell'
2.	tá:pan	'split'	11.	číhaŋ	'hire'
3.	hídoḍ	'cook'	12.	tóɲi	'become hot'
4.	čɨkid	'vaccinate'	13.	wíḍut	'swing'
5.	gátwid	'shoot'	14.	tá:taḍ	'feet'
6.	čúku	'become black'	15.	kí:čud	'build a house for'
7.	dágṣp	'press with hand'	16.	dó:dom	'copulate'
8.	tóha	'become white'	17.	tá:tam	'touch'
9.	ǰú:kĭ	'rain' (noun)			

Proto-Bantu Voiced Obstruents

The following set of data is from Proto-Bantu—the reconstructed latest common ancestor of the modern Bantu languages spoken in Eastern, Central, and Southern Africa, including Swahili and Ganda. [β, l, γ] are in complementary distribution with [b, d, g] respectively. Account for their distribution by postulating an underlying phoneme for each pair and stating the rule accounting for the phonetic forms.

1.	βale	'two'	13.	kiγa	'eyebrow'
2.	leme	'tongue'	14.	γiγε	'locust'
3.	taβe	'twig'	15.	kulu	'tortoise'
4.	pala	'antelope'	16.	oŋgo	'cooking pot'
5.	kondε	'bean'	17.	tεndε	'palm tree'
6.	zɔŋgɔ	'gall'	18.	zala	'hunger'
7.	βεγa	'monkey'	19.	zɔγu	'elephant'
8.	βεmbe	'pigeon'	20.	βele	'body'
9.	limo	'god, spirit'	21.	lεlu	'chin, beard'
10.	kaŋga	'guinea fowl'	22.	eγi	'water'
11.	γɔmbε	'cattle'	23.	kiŋgɔ	'neck'
12.	lelɔ	'fire'	24.	nto	'person'

Voiced Stops in Lowland Murut

In Lowland Murut the voiced stops [b, d, g] are in complementary distribution with the sounds [β, ɾ, γ], respectively. State the rule that defines their distribution.

1.	maŋúɾaɾ	'will scrub'	16.	indáγu	'speak!'
2.	áβaγ	'loincloth'	17.	lumɔ́ŋgɔ?	'will cease'
3.	pálaɾ	'palm of the hand'	18.	bálɔy	'house'
4.	sɔ́ɾɔy	'remain'	19.	iŋgɔ́nɔm	'six times'
5.	inúmɔ? γítiɔ	'drink this!'	20.	malá:t dálanti	'the road is bad'
6.	kakáβil	'paddle'	21.	maγambáyɔy	'bullock'
7.	páliγ	'poison for blowpipe darts'	22.	bú:k	'rotten egg'
			23.	dáiti	'just now'
8.	iγɔ́ndɔ?	'once'	24.	iŋgálan	'name'
9.	giγiúl	'wooden spatula'	25.	maŋándɔy	'will work'
10.	maγálaw	'will commit adultery'	26.	gítiɔ	'this'
11.	má:luɾ	'distant'	27.	mambála?	'will inform'
12.	nakaβála?	'has informed'	28.	anak ditúnu	'Tunu's child'
13.	áma? ritúnu	'Tunu's father'	29.	mɔlɔ́ndɔm gíti	'it's dark here'
14.	mɔ́:nsɔy γíti	'it's good here'	30.	mapísɔk bálɔyti	'the house is cramped'
15.	mapísɔktɔ:ʃɔ βálɔyti	'the house is really cramped'			

Mohawk Stops

Mohawk has six phonetic oral stops (as well as a glottal stop, which we will disregard here). The bilabial stops are rare and for the most part restricted to recent loan words. Decide which of the following two hypotheses is correct:

Hypothesis A. Mohawk has the six distinct oral stop phonemes /p b t d k g/.

Hypothesis B. Mohawk has only three distinct oral stop phonemes in its underlying phoneme inventory.

If you select hypothesis A, show that the inventory of stop phonemes cannot be reduced, by citing (near-)minimal pairs. If you select hypothesis B, show that it is correct by (a) listing the phonemes, and (b) listing each variant (surface reflex) of each phoneme together with the context in which it occurs. (Assume that the data is complete in all relevant respects.)

1.	oli:de?	'pigeon'	8.	oya:gala	'shirt'
2.	zahset	'hide it!' (sg.)	9.	ohyotsah	'chin'
3.	ga:lis	'stocking'	10.	labahbet	'catfish'
4.	odahsa	'tail'	11.	sdu:ha	'a little bit'
5.	wisk	'five'	12.	jiks	'fly'
6.	degeni	'two'	13.	desda?n	'stand up!' (sg.)
7.	aplam	'Abram, Abraham'	14.	de:zekw	'pick it up!' (sg.)

Squamish Vowels

Squamish has the following stops, fricatives and liquids.

	stop		fricative	lateral
labials:	p	p'		
dentals:	t	t'	s	
	c	c'		
palatals:	č	č'	š	
laterals:	ƛ	ƛ'		1
velars:	kʷ	k'ʷ	xʷ	
	k	k'		
uvulars:	qʷ	q'ʷ	χʷ	
	q	q'	χ	

Notes. [ł] is an allophone of /l/ occurring in non-word-initial position. /c, c', č, č'/ are affricates. /ƛ, ƛ'/ are laterally released stops.

Show that the phones [e·], [e], [ε·], and [εy] derive from a single underlying phoneme. State the rules accounting for their occurrence, and indicate any necessary ordering.

1.	ce?	'there is'	16.	χε·q	'scratch'
2.	q'εyt	'be morning'	17.	če·ƛ	'top'
3.	t'ε·qʷ	'cold'	18.	q'ε·χεy?	'become black'
4.	χʷε·q'ʷ	'be arrested'	19.	tme·xʷ	'earth, ground'
5.	χεyp'	'get touched'	20.	qle·m	'weak'
6.	ce·xʷ	'reach'	21.	sq'εy?	'slices of dried salmon'
7.	tse?	'feel cold'	22.	χʷεy?	'be lost'
8.	k'ʷe·n	'few'	23.	ne?č	'high seas'
9.	wε·łq'ʷt	'ask'	24.	kʷce?c	'person with magic power'
10.	te·	'this'	25.	slε·ł	'bunch of blankets'
11.	nəq'e·łos	'wise'	26.	χʷε·ł? ·	'come out'
12.	xʷałεytn	'white man'	27.	nsqεynm̥	'rub oil in one's hair'
13.	le·xʷ	'fall'	28.	stæqtaqεyw	'horses'
14.	ƛ'ε·q	'arrive'	29.	mε·χæƛ	'black bear'
15.	?e·	'be here'			

Multiple Complementation in Thai

The set of obstruents in Thai is fully exemplified in the following examples. Determine the set of obstruent phonemes in Thai. Do [p', t', k'] represent distinct obstruent phonemes, or are they surface variants of other phonemes? If so, which ones? Justify your choice (if the evidence is insufficient on the basis of criteria established so far, suggest what criteria might lead to the appropriate choice.)

Notes. [p', t', k'] are unreleased voiceless stops. No words begin with [g].

1.	bil	'Bill'	24.	müü	'hand'
2.	saam	'three'	25.	ŋən	'silver'
3.	yaa	'medicine'	26.	hɔɔ	'package'
4.	rak'	'love'	27.	baa	'crazy'
5.	loŋ	'go down'	28.	brüü	'extremely fast'
6.	haa	'five'	29.	plaa	'fish'
7.	dii	'good'	30.	caan	'dish'
8.	tʰee	'pour'	31.	tʰruumɛɛn	'Truman'
9.	kʰɛŋ	'hard'	32.	panyaa	'brains'
10.	ləəy	'pass'	33.	pʰyaa	[title]
11.	lüak'	'choose'	34.	klaaŋ	'middle'
12.	cʰat'	'clear'	35.	traa	'stamp'
13.	riip'	'hurry'	36.	ɔɔk'	'exit'
14.	pʰrɛɛ	'silk cloth'	37.	kiə	'wooden shoes'
15.	kʰwaa	'right side'	38.	kɛɛ	'old'
16.	dray	'drive' (golf)	39.	düŋ	'pull'
17.	kan	'ward off'	40.	cuək'	'pure white'
18.	pʰleeŋ	'song'	41.	cʰan	'me'
19.	staaŋ	'money'	42.	rap'	'take'
20.	yiisip'	'twenty'	43.	pʰaa	'cloth'
21.	kʰaa	'kill'	44.	dam	'black'
22.	raay	'case'	45.	tit'	'get stuck'
23.	sip'	'ten'	46.	pen	'alive'

A Research Problem

This problem asks you to conduct some research on your own. Make up a problem (of the sort we have presented above) which sets out data illustrating a phonological rule in a non-European language. Use the following format:

- Title

- Brief account of the scope of the problem, with explanation of any unfamiliar symbols, etc.

- Data (use the format that seems appropriate)

- Statement of the task

Try to use the minimum amount of data sufficient to lead the person working the problem to the correct solution. Check to make sure that there are not two solutions consistent with the data, one of which could be eliminated if a little further data were provided.

3. Natural Classes of Sounds

English Plurals

The following is a list of some singular nouns in English:

lip, rock, tree, latch, gum, myth, laugh, two, cove, toe, bell, wretch, rib, load, breeze, fudge, hen, law, fez, bar, bat, tea, garage, turf, lash, row, lunch, tray, tag, stick, hinge, witch.

When you form the plural of these words you will notice that the plural marker is pronounced in three different ways, according to the word. These different pronunciations can be represented as follows: [-ɪz] as in bus*es*, [-s] as in rock*s*, and [-z] as in tree*s*.

1. Divide the nouns above into three sets according to the plural ending they take: that is, into words that take [-ɪz], words that take [-s], and words that take [-z].

2. If you are a native speaker of English, or know English reasonably well, this problem should have been easy for you. You should have no trouble forming the correct plural of nouns like those above when you see or hear the singular. It is part of your knowledge of English to produce the correct plurals without hesitation. Suppose we ask the question: how do speakers of English do this? Or in other words, in what form do speakers of English internalize their knowledge of plural formation? We may consider four possibilities:

Hypothesis A.   They memorize the plural form for every noun they come across.

Hypothesis B.   They learn the plural form on the basis of spelling. For instance, they learn that words that end with the letter *p* in the singular form the plural by adding [-s].

Hypothesis C.   They know that the sound (rather than the letter) in which the singular ends determines the pronunciation of the plural ending. They have thus memorized a list of English speech sounds that will be followed by the plural ending [-s], another list that will be followed by [-z], and a third list that will be followed by [-ɪz].

Hypothesis D.   They know that if the singular ends in a sound of a certain type, the plural ending will be [-s], that if it ends in a sound of another type it will be [-z], and that if it ends in a sound of a third type it will be [-ɪz]. In other words, the speakers have not memorized three lists of speech sounds for the purpose of plural formation. Rather, they learn which sound types (or *classes*) are relevant.

Think about Hypotheses A—D and try to eliminate as many as you can. It should be easy to eliminate two of them. You may be able to eliminate a third if you think about it for a while.

Classes of Sounds

1. Observe the British and American pronunciations of the following words. In the right-hand column, transcribe the words as they are pronounced in American English, for example in your own speech, or that of a friend.

		British	American
1.	pure	pyuə	
2.	cute	kyuːt	
3.	tune	tyuːn	
4.	abuse	əbyuːz	
5.	dues	dyuːz	
6.	argue	ɑːgyuː	
7.	muse	myuːz	
8.	new	nyuː	
9.	lewd	lyuːd	
10.	few	fyuː	
11.	view	vyuː	
12.	enthuse	ɪnθyuːz	
13.	suit	syuːt	
14.	hue	hyuː	

2. State the context(s) in which British [yu] is replaced by American [u]. If possible, state the context as a *class* of sounds, rather than listing individual phonemes.

71

Distinctive Features of American English

This exercise is designed as a way of testing your knowledge of the feature system. First, review the classification of sounds given in the Chart of Distinctive Features, page 33. Then fill in the values for each of the features below without referring to the chart.

	i	o	ʊ	u	ɑ	æ	w	y	p	m	v	θ	d	s	n	l	č	ž	r	k
syllabic																				
sonorant																				
high																				
back																				
low																				
coronal																				
anterior																				
labial																				
nasal																				
lateral																				
continuant																				
voiced																				
strident																				

Are the features given in the above chart sufficient to differentiate all English phonemes listed? If not, what additional feature(s) would be needed to distinguish all the phonemes of English?

73

English /aw/

1. List all the English consonants which may appear after /aw/ in monosyllabic words, with an example of each. (An example is given.)

    /t/   shout

2. Identify the class of English consonants that is *excluded* in this position.

Natural Classes

1. Each of the following groups of sounds consists of members of a natural class of sounds, plus one sound that is not a member of that class.

   a. Identify the sound that is not a member of the class.

   b. Name the feature(s) that define the class to which the remaining sounds belong. (In some cases there will be more than one choice. You are asked to find only one.)

       i.   [kʷ, v, p, r, f, m]

       ii.   [p, n, g, b, č, š, m]

       iii.   [f, g, n, p, d, m]

       iv.   [e, a, i, æ, ɛ]

       v.   [n, l, ã, z, r, h]

2. Each circle or box in the following charts encloses a natural class. Describe each of these natural classes in terms of features. Use the *minimum* specification necessary for describing each class. (Consider [ɯ] as a back unrounded vowel with the same tongue configuration as [u].)

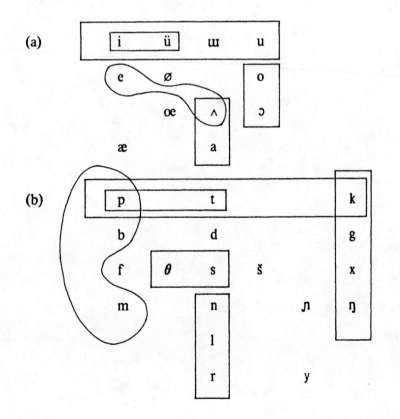

Initial Consonant Clusters in English

1. Not all consonants of English may appear in word-initial clusters after /s/. List, according to point of articulation, those consonants that *may* appear in this position, with a word exemplifying each one. (Make your list as complete as you can.)

2. Can any of the consonants you have listed in part 1 be grouped into natural classes? If so, identify these classes in terms of the minimal set of distinctive features required to completely identify them.

3. Identify the consonants that may occur word-initially between /s/ and another consonant (that is, medially in three-member clusters). What natural class do they constitute? Is this the same as one of the classes you identified in part 2?

Consonant Clusters in Cambodian

Cambodian words may begin with a variety of consonant clusters, as the following word lists illustrate.

Notes. /p t c k/ are unaspirated. /Ch/ represents the sequence /C+h/.

A.   CC clusters with no transitional sound:

1.	praə	'to use'		11.	psaa	'market'
2.	phək	'to drink'		12.	trəy	'fish'
3.	thaa	'to say'		13.	craən	'much, many'
4.	chaa	'to fry'		14.	kraw	'outside'
5.	ksac	'sand'		15.	khae	'month, moon'
6.	spɨy	'cabbage'		16.	stɨŋ	'river'
7.	skŏəl	'acquainted with'		17.	smaw	'grass'
8.	snaa	'crossbow'		18.	sɲaeɲ	'to fear'
9.	sɲiəm	'quiet'		19.	swaa	'monkey'
10.	slap	'to die'		20.	srəy	'woman'

B.   CʰC clusters (first member aspirated):

1.	pʰtĕəh	'house'		17.	pʰcŏəp	'to attach'
2.	pʰkaa	'flower'		18.	pʰnum	'mountain'
3.	pʰɲaə	'to send'		19.	pʰŋuut	'to bathe'
4.	pʰyuə	'to suspend'		20.	pʰləw	'road, way'
5.	tʰpŏəl	'cheek'		21.	tʰkaəŋ	'illustrious'
6.	tʰməy	'new'		22.	tʰnam	'herb'
7.	tʰŋay	'day, sun'		23.	tʰwiə	'door, opening'
8.	tʰyuuŋ	'charcoal'		24.	tʰlĕə?	'to fall'
9.	cʰpuŋ	'to inhale'		25.	cʰkae	'dog'
10.	cʰmaa	'cat'		26.	cʰnaŋ	'kettle'
11.	cʰŋaay	'distant'		27.	cʰweiŋ	'left side'
12.	cʰlaɑŋ	'to cross'		28.	kʰpŭəh	'to be high'
13.	kʰtĕəh	'skillet'		29.	kʰcəy	'to borrow, lend'
14.	kʰmae	'Khmer'		30.	kʰnoŋ	'in, inside'
15.	kʰɲom	'I, my, me'		31.	kʰwa?	'to be blind'
16.	kʰyɑl	'wind, air'		32.	kʰliən	'to be hungry'

C. C^əC clusters (with transitional schwa):

1.	pᵊʔaem	'to be sweet'	17.	pᵊɗəy	'husband'
2.	tᵊʔouɲ	'to whine'	18.	tᵊɓaaɲ	'to weave'
3.	cᵊʔəŋ	'bone'	19.	cᵊɓah	'to be clear'
4.	cᵊɗao	'ingot'	20.	kᵊʔaaʔ	'to cough'
5.	kᵊɓaal	'head'	21.	kᵊɗaw	'to be hot'
6.	kᵊŋaan	'goose'	22.	sᵊʔaek	'tomorrow'
7.	sᵊɓəw	'thatch'	23.	sᵊɗap	'to listen'
8.	ʔᵊwəy	'what'	24.	mᵊteeh	'a pepper'
9.	mᵊcul	'needle'	25.	mᵊʔaap	'an herb'
10.	mᵊɗaay	'mother'	26.	mᵊnŏəh	'pineapple'
11.	mᵊɲae-mɲaa	'plaintively'	27.	mᵊlup	'shade'
12.	mᵊriəm	'finger, toe'	28.	mᵊsaw	'flour'
13.	mᵊhoup	'food'	29.	lᵊʔaa	'good, pretty'
14.	lᵊɓaeŋ	'game'	30.	lᵊmɔɔm	'sufficient'
15.	lᵊɲiəc	'afternoon'	31.	lᵊwɛɛŋ	'compartment'
16.	lᵊhoŋ	'papaya'			

1. List all consonants occurring as the second member of a cluster.

2. List all consonants occurring as the first member of a cluster. Which consonants are missing in this position?

3. Identify the phonological conditions determining whether a given cluster falls into set A, B, or C above. Use distinctive features to identify natural classes whenever possible.

Turkish Vowels

The following examples illustrate alternations in Turkish suffixes after each of the vowel phonemes of Turkish.

		nom. sg.	gen. sg.	nom. pl.	gen. pl.
1.	'rope'	ip	ipin	ipler	iplerin
2.	'girl'	kɨz	kɨzɨn	kɨzlar	kɨzlarɨn
3.	'face'	yüz	yüzün	yüzler	yüzlerin
4.	'stamp'	pul	pulun	pullar	pullarɨn
5.	'hand'	el	elin	eller	ellerin
6.	'bell'	čan	čanɨn	čanlar	čanlarɨn
7.	'village'	köy	köyün	köyler	köylerin
8.	'end'	son	sonun	sonlar	sonlarɨn

1. Give a distinctive feature characterization of each of the vowels of Turkish:

   i   ɨ   ü   u   e   a   ö   o

   high

   back

   rounded

2. Identify each alternant of the suffixes:

   genitive:

   plural:

3. State the rules that determine the quality of suffix vowels in Turkish, using distinctive features (you should be able to account for all forms with two rules).

Welsh Consonant Mutation

In Welsh, word-initial consonants exhibit alternations in certain grammatical contexts. Three series are found. Phonetic, rather than orthographic transcriptions are given.

Notes. The terms "nasalized", "aspirated", and "lenited" are traditional denominations for the three series and do not necessarily indicate true phonetic properties. "Ø" is the null symbol.

	citation form	nasalized series	aspirated series	lenited series
1.	p	m̥	f	b
2.	t	n̥	θ	d
3.	k	ŋ̥	x	g
4.	b	m	b	v
5.	d	n	d	ð
6.	g	ŋ	g	Ø
7.	m	m	m	v
8.	l̥	l̥	l̥	l
9.	r̥	r̥	r̥	r
10.	s	s	s	s
11.	n	n	n	n

Write separate rules accounting for the mutated consonants that appear in each series. Your rules should derive each series separately from the citation form. Use distinctive feature notation wherever classes of sounds are involved. In the lenited series, [ɣ] can be taken as an intermediate stage between [g] and Ø.

1. State the rule for the "nasalized" series.

2. State the rule for the "aspirated" series.

3. State the rules for the "lenited" series. (Note: a few general rules are to be preferred to many specific ones.)

Sanskrit Retroflexion

In Sanskrit, the dental nasal [n] becomes retroflex [ṇ] if a vowel or n, m, y, or w follow, and if moreover, within the same word one of the sounds ṣ, r, ṛ, ṝ precedes the n immediately or else is separated from it by any number of vowels, velars, labials, h or y.

Assume that the nonsyllabic segments which appear in phonological representations when this rule applies fall into the taxonomic classes indicated in the following table:

	labial	dental	retroflex	palato-alveolar	velar	glottal
stops:	p	t	ṭ	č	k	
	p^h	t^h	$ṭ^h$	$č^h$	k^h	
	b	d	ḍ	ǰ	g	
	b^h	d^h	$ḍ^h$	$ǰ^h$	g^h	
fricatives:		s	ṣ	š		
nasals:	m	n				
approximants:		l	r	y	w	h

1. Present a distinctive feature chart of Sanskrit consonants.

2. Restate the rule in question using distinctive features to designate natural classes.

4. Phonological Rules

The Formalism of Phonological Rules

Phonological rules are usually written in the following form:

$$A \rightarrow B / C \underline{\quad} D$$

where the following conditions are satisfied:

1. A, B, C, D are distinctive feature matrices except that:

    - A or B (but not both) may be the null set Ø
    - C or D (or both) may be absent
    - A consists of only one feature column

    If C and D are both absent, the rule is said to be *context-free*. Otherwise, the rule is *context-sensitive*.

2. C and D may contain (or consist solely of) the boundary symbols # (word boundary) and + (morpheme boundary).

In such rules, A is said to be the *affected segment*, B is the *change*, and C and D constitute the *context* or *environment*. CAD constitutes the *structural description* (SD) of the rule, and CBD constitutes the *structural change* (SC).

Example. The rule "/b d g/ become the corresponding continuants [β ð γ] in intervocalic position" is expressed as follows:

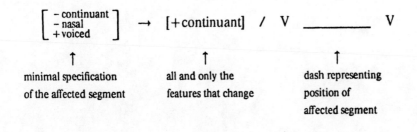

| minimal specification of the affected segment | all and only the features that change | dash representing position of affected segment |

Some conventional symbols:

Ø the null set
      Ø → B / C ___ D "insert B between C and D"
      A → Ø / C ___ D "delete A between C and D"
\# word boundary
\+ morpheme boundary
C [−syllabic] segment
V [+syllabic] segment
V́ stressed vowel
C_0 zero or more [−syllabic] segments

Writing Phonological Rules

1. State what the following rules do in plain English:

   a. $[+\text{nas}] \rightarrow \emptyset \;/\; [+\text{syl}] \underline{\quad} \#$

   b. $\begin{bmatrix} +\text{syl} \\ +\text{high} \end{bmatrix} \rightarrow [-\text{syl}] \;/\; \underline{\quad} [+\text{syl}]$

   c. $\emptyset \rightarrow \begin{bmatrix} +\text{syl} \\ +\text{high} \\ -\text{back} \end{bmatrix} \;/\; \begin{bmatrix} +\text{strident} \\ +\text{coronal} \end{bmatrix} + \underline{\quad} \begin{bmatrix} -\text{sonorant} \\ +\text{coronal} \end{bmatrix}$

   d. $\begin{bmatrix} -\text{sonorant} \\ -\text{continuant} \\ -\text{labial} \end{bmatrix} \rightarrow [-\text{back}] \;/\; \underline{\quad} \begin{bmatrix} +\text{syl} \\ -\text{back} \\ +\text{high} \end{bmatrix}$

   e. $V \rightarrow [+\text{stress}] \;/\; \underline{\quad} C_0 \, V \, C_0 \, V \, C_0 \#$

2. Restate the following rules in formal notation:

   a. The glide [y] is inserted between a high front vowel and any following vowel.

   b. A voiced consonant becomes nasal after a nasal stop.

   c. Obstruents are devoiced word-finally or when they precede voiceless obstruents.

   d. A stressed vowel is lengthened if the following vowel is unstressed.

   e. The vowels [ʌ, a] are rounded if the preceding syllable contains a stressed rounded vowel.

   f. Voiced stops become the corresponding fricatives intervocalically.

Turkish Possessives

In the set of data below, the vowel of the possessed form suffix assimilates to the quality of the preceding stem vowel, according to the rule of vowel harmony. (See the problem "Turkish Vowels", above.)

Notice the alternation involving the final consonant of the noun stem in some of the forms:

		noun stem	possessed form	UR (stem)
1.	'rope'	ip	ipi	
2.	'louse'	bit	biti	
3.	'reason'	sebep	sebebi	
4.	'wing'	kanat	kanadɨ	
5.	'honor'	šeref	šerefi	
6.	'rump'	kɨč	kɨčɨ	
7.	'pilot'	pilot	pilotu	
8.	'bunch'	demet	demeti	
9.	'wine'	šarap	šarabɨ	
10.	'Ahmed'	ahmet	ahmedi	
11.	'slipper'	pabuč	pabuǰu	
12.	'power'	güč	güǰü	
13.	'basket'	sepet	sepeti	
14.	'art'	sanat	sanatɨ	
15.	'cap'	kep	kepi	
16.	'worm'	kurt	kurdu	
17.	'hair'	sač	sačɨ	
18.	'color'	renk	rengi	

1. Give the underlying representation (UR) of the noun stems in the space provided.

2. Write the phonological rule that accounts for the consonant alternations.

3. Justify your rule by suggesting an alternative and showing that it is inferior to your solution.

More Phonological Rules

Restate the rules you formulated in Part Two of this book in terms of the notation explained in "Phonological Rules", for the following languages:

1. Angas

2. Kongo

3. Ewe

4. Ganda

5. Papago

6. Proto-Bantu

7. Lowland Murut

8. Mohawk

9. Squamish

Abbreviatory Conventions (I)

A rule *schema* (plural: *schemata*) is an abbreviation of two or more rules that share portions of their environment. Sequences of rules are collapsed into rule schemata by means of certain abbreviatory conventions.

A. **The Parenthesis Notation**

If two rules are related in such a way that the environment of one is properly included in the environment of the other, and if no other rule is ordered between these two rules, they may be collapsed by the use of parentheses.

Consider the following two rules:

R_1: $A \rightarrow B / C D \_\_\_ E$

R_2: $A \rightarrow B / \ C \_\_\_ E$

The environment of R_2 is properly included in the environment of R_1. These two rules may be collapsed into the following schema:

S_1: $A \rightarrow B / C (D) \_\_\_ E$

We say that the schema S_1 *expands* as the two rules R_1, R_2 in that order (with the longer rule preceding the shorter).

B. **The Brace Notation**

If two rules are related in such a way that they share continuous parts of their environment, and if no other rule is ordered between these two rules, they may be collapsed by the use of braces.

Consider the following two rules:

R_3: $A \rightarrow B / C \_\_\_ D$

R_4: $A \rightarrow B / C \_\_\_ E$

These two rules share portion "C" of their environment, and collapse into the following schema:

S_2: $A \rightarrow B / C \_\_\_ \begin{Bmatrix} D \\ E \end{Bmatrix}$

We say that schema S_2 *expands* as the two rules R_3, R_4 in that order (with the upper elements in braces selected before the lower elements).

Using Abbreviatory Conventions

1. Expand the following rule schemata into sequences of rules:

   a. $A \rightarrow B / \underline{\hspace{1cm}} (C(\{ \begin{smallmatrix} D \\ E \end{smallmatrix} \})) F$

   b. $A \rightarrow B / \{ \begin{smallmatrix} C \\ (D)E \end{smallmatrix} \} \underline{\hspace{1cm}} (F) G$

2. Collapse the following rules into a single rule schema:

   a. $A \rightarrow B / \underline{\hspace{1cm}} DEG$

   b. $A \rightarrow B / \underline{\hspace{1cm}} EFG$

   c. $A \rightarrow B / \underline{\hspace{1cm}} EG$

   d. $A \rightarrow B / \underline{\hspace{1cm}} DEFG$

3. Can the following rules be collapsed into a single rule schema? If so, state the schema.

   a. $A \rightarrow B / C \underline{\hspace{1cm}} D$

   b. $A \rightarrow B / \underline{\hspace{1cm}} DE$

   c. $A \rightarrow B / C \underline{\hspace{1cm}} E$

Tibetan Numerals

The following forms illustrate a process of word formation in modern Tibetan (Lhasa dialect). In the transcriptions, the difference between sh and s̱ẖ, g and g̱ may be ignored.

Note. The items ǰugǰig and ǰuŋa are actually pronounced [ǰugǰɨ] and [ǰöːŋa]. We shall assume that these pronunciations are due to further, independent phonological processes not of concern here. They may be ignored for the purposes of the present problem.

UR:

1.	ǰu	'ten'
2.	ǰig	'one'
3.	ǰugǰig	'eleven'
4.	s̱ẖi	'four'
5.	ǰubshi	'fourteen'
6.	s̱ẖibǰu	'forty'
7.	g̱u	'nine'
8.	ǰurgu	'nineteen'
9.	g̱ubǰu	'ninety'
10.	ŋa	'five'
11.	ǰuŋa	'fifteen'
12.	ŋabǰu	'fifty'

1. List the morphemes associated with each of the following meanings. Give all alternants.

    'ten'

    'one'

    'four'

    'nine'

    'five'

2. What is the order of morphemes in the Tibetan numeral?

    teens (11, 14, 15, 19):

    tens (40, 50, 90):

3. The simplest way of describing these forms is to set up an underlying representation (UR) for each word consisting of the base form of each of its morphemes. All forms can be derived from this UR by a regular phonological change. Note that the UR need not be identical to any actually appearing word. Determine the UR of each of the words listed above and write it in the space provided. What is the phonological change?

Consonant Dissimilation in Kikuyu

1. Determine the base form of the infinitive prefix in Kikuyu, and state the rule that accounts for its pattern of alternation.

1.	γoteŋera	'to run'	12.	kohɛtoka	'to pass'
2.	γokuua	'to carry'	13.	koγamba	'to make a sound'
3.	γokoora	'to root out'	14.	koniina	'to finish'
4.	koruγa	'to cook'	15.	γoita	'to strangle'
5.	kooria	'to ask'	16.	γokuɲa	'to pinch'
6.	komɛɲa	'to know'	17.	koγuuta	'to comb'
7.	kohɔta	'to be able'	18.	kohɛ	'to give'
8.	γocina	'to burn'	19.	koina	'to dance'
9.	koγeera	'to fetch'	20.	γoɗɛka	'to laugh'
10.	γoɗaaka	'to play'	21.	koγaya	'to divide out'
11.	γocuuka	'to slander'	22.	γokaya	'to cut into strips'

2. Determine the underlying form of the prefixes illustrated in the examples below, and explain their pattern of alternation.

23.	kerɔrirɛ moanakɛ	'it (crab) looked at the boy'	28.	γeγakarɔra	'it will look at it' (baby)
24.	kemorɔrirɛ	'it looked at him'	29.	γeγaγekarɔra	'and so it will look at it'
25.	γekamorɔra	'it will look at him'	30.	γeγaγeγakuɲa	'and so it will pinch it'
26.	γeγakemorɔra	'and so it will look at him'	31.	γeγakemokuɲa	'and so it will pinch him'
27.	γekarɔra kaana	'it will look at the baby'			

3. State the rules by which velar stops are adapted into Kikuyu from English. (Do not be concerned with other correspondences.)

32.	ŋga:βana	'governor'	40.	kaarati	'carrot'
33.	ɲjaγi	'jug'	41.	kwinini	'quinine'
34.	kaɲjo	'council'	42.	mbureki	'brake'
35.	ŋgaamu	'gum'	43.	mbaγiti	'packet'
36.	ŋgaati	'guard'	44.	γaaki	'khaki'
37.	ndiγiri	'degree'	45.	iγɔɔti	'coat'
38.	kambe	'camp'	46.	ɗiγwɔta	'squatter'
39.	ŋgiya	'gear'	47.	ɗunaγɔɔγi	'synagogue'

Abbreviatory Conventions (II)

Processes of assimilation are characterized by the fact that a given sound adapts in some of its features to those of another sound in the sequence. Thus, for example, the English plural suffix appears as voiceless [s] after nouns ending with a voiceless sound and as voiced [z] after nouns ending with a voiced sound, as illustrated by such words as *caps, coughs, cats, baths, cakes,* vs. *cubs, caves, cads, lathes, cogs.*

To capture the fact that assimilations of this type are unitary processes we may extend the notation so as to allow the coefficient of the different features to be represented not only by constant values such as + or − but also by variables that range over the values + or −. Customarily, Greek letters $\alpha \ \beta \ \gamma \ \delta$ have been used to represent these variables. In the extended notation a rule like the English plural rule could be formulated as follows:

$$\begin{bmatrix} - \text{ sonorant} \\ + \text{coronal} \\ + \text{strident} \\ + \text{continuant} \end{bmatrix} \rightarrow \quad [\alpha \text{ voiced}] \, / \, [\alpha \text{ voiced}] \underline{\quad}$$

This rule schema is expanded into rules by first replacing all occurrences of "α" with "+", then replacing them with "−". This gives the following two expansions:

$$\begin{bmatrix} - \text{ sonorant} \\ + \text{coronal} \\ + \text{strident} \\ + \text{continuant} \end{bmatrix} \rightarrow \quad [+ \text{ voiced}] \, / \, [+ \text{ voiced}] \underline{\quad}$$

$$\begin{bmatrix} - \text{ sonorant} \\ + \text{coronal} \\ + \text{strident} \\ + \text{continuant} \end{bmatrix} \rightarrow \quad [- \text{ voiced}] \, / \, [- \text{ voiced}] \underline{\quad}$$

Voicing Assimilation in Russian Prepositions

State the rule accounting for the consonantal alternations in the prepositions illustrated below.

		'from'	'without'	'next to'
1.	'rose'	at rózɨ	bʸiz rózɨ	u rózɨ
2.	'Ala' (name)	at álɨ	bʸiz álɨ	u álɨ
3.	'cow'	at karóvɨ	bʸis karóvɨ	u karóvɨ
4.	'beard'	ad baradɨ̀	bʸiz baradɨ̀	u baradɨ̀
5.	'sister'	at sʸistrɨ̀	bʸis sʸistrɨ̀	u sʸistrɨ̀

5. Rule Systems

Rule Ordering in Klamath

In the "Morphophonemics" chapter of his *Klamath Grammar*, Barker lists a number of rules that account for the phonetic shape of Klamath words. Among them are (A)—(E):

Note. The change of [y] to [i] in the form given in B is accounted for by a separate rule not at issue here.

A. nl → ll

   /honli:na/ → holli:na   'flies along the bank'

B. nḷ → lh

   /honly/ → holhi   'flies into'

C. nl' → l?

   /honl'a:l'a/ → hol?a:l'a   'flies into the fire'

D. lḷ → lh

   /pa:lḷa/ → pa:lha   'dries on'

E. ll' → l?

   /yalyall'i/ → yalyal?i   'clear'

In his grammar, Barker makes the following assumptions:

> Phonological rules are unordered. All rules apply simultaneously to underlying representations to derive surface representations.

Show how Barker's set of rules can be simplified by abandoning these assumptions and assuming that phonological rules apply in order, each rule applying to the output of the preceding rule in the list of ordered rules. Write the rules sufficient to describe the above data, and state the order in which they apply.

Rule Ordering in Russian

The forms below illustrate some characteristic alternations in Russian. As we see from Data I, the past suffix is -*l*, the feminine suffix is -*a*, and the plural suffix is -*i* and causes $l \rightarrow l^y$.

The verb roots are obtained by subtracting the suffixes. Thus the past feminine of 'return' consists of the root $v^y irnu$- and the suffixes -*l* and -*a*. The verb roots of Data I(a) end in vowels, while those of Data I(b) end in consonants.

Data I

	1st. sg. present	past masc.	past fem.	past pl.	
a.	v^yirnú	v^yirnúl	v^yirnúla	v^yirnúl^{y}i	'return (s. th.)'
	vrú	vrál	vralá	vrál^{y}i	'lie, mislead'
	stayú	stayál	stayála	stayál^{y}i	'stand'
b.	p^yikú	p^yók	p^yiklá	p^yikl^{y}í	'bake'
	v^yizú	v^yós	v^yizlá	v^yizl^{y}í	'transport'
	magú	mók	maglá	magl^{y}í	'can'
	móknu	mók	mókla	mókl^{y}i	'soak'

Data II

p^yók l^{y}i	'whether he baked'	v^yós l^{y}i	'whether he carried'
p^yóg bɨ	'were he to bake'	v^yóz bɨ	'were he to carry'

mók l^{y}i	'whether he could/soaked'
móg bɨ	'were he to be able/soak'

Under the assumption that phonological rules apply *simultaneously* to underlying representations, the consonantal alternations illustrated above can be described by the following set of rules:

1. Word-final /l/ in a verb is replaced by Ø (the zero element) after a consonant.

2. An obstruent is voiceless if it is word-final, or followed by final /l/ in a verb, unless it is immediately followed in the next word by a voiced obstruent.

3. An obstruent agrees in voicing with an obstruent which immediately follows it in the next word, or which is separated from it by word-final /l/ in a verb.

It will be noticed that rules 1—3 contain some redundancy, since some rules repeat conditions that are stated by other rules. Show how this redundancy can be eliminated by restating rules 1—3 as *ordered* rules, that is, rules that apply to underlying representations in a stipulated order.

A Children's Language

Two brothers living with their parents in Cambridge, Massachusetts, aged 4 and 5.5, were observed to speak a dialect of English deviating in certain respects from the adult norm. This dialect was the only language spoken by these children, and they used it in communicating with each other, with adults, and with their playmates. Their oldest brother, who understood this dialect, served as translator in situations in which they could not communicate effectively with adults. Apart from the differences in pronunciation illustrated below, the grammar of the children's dialect was almost exactly the same as the grammar of the dialect of the adult community.

	adult word	children's word		adult word	children's word
1.	puppy	pəʔiy	14.	died	day?
2.	kick	kı?	15.	took	teykɨʔ/tʊk
3.	baby	beyʔiy	16.	bit	bɪt
4.	walks	wɑkt	17.	talked	tɑkɨʔ
5.	walked	wɑkt	18.	daddy	dæʔiy
6.	ran	rɔnd	19.	Bobby	bɑʔiy
7.	men	mænd	20.	tag	tæg
8.	pet	pɛt	21.	paper	peyʔər
9.	can (3. p. sg.)	kænd	22.	takes	teykt
10.	did	dı?	23.	dogs	dɑgd
11.	does	dəd	24.	toot	tuw?
12.	talks	tɑkt	25.	suit	tuwt
13.	beat	biyt	26.	cake	key?

1. What rules distinguish the children's phonology from the phonology of the adult community?

2. Must they be stated in a particular order? If so, why?

Derivations

A *derivation* is a sequence of lines such that the following conditions are satisfied:

1. the first line is an underlying representation (UR) consisting of the distinctive feature matrices that describe the fully-inflected forms of words;

2. each successive line is derived from the preceding one by the application of a phonological rule;

3. all phonological rules are applied in the order given (no rule applies out of turn);

4. the final line is the surface representation (SR) or phonetic form.

The *input* to a rule is the phonological representation which is scanned for possible application of the rule. The *output* of a rule is the phonological representation that results from applying the rule to an input that satisfies its structural description.

Example: Consider a language with the following two rules:

$$A: V \rightarrow \emptyset \, / \, [+\text{sonorant}] \, \underline{\quad} \, \#$$

$$B: [+\text{nasal}] \rightarrow \emptyset \, / \, \underline{\quad} \, \#$$

This set of rules will apply to the underlying representation *pana* to produce the surface representation *pa*. The derivation is as follows:

/pana/	UR
pan	by rule A
pa	by rule B

Notice that *pana* is the input to rule A and *pan* is its output. Similarly *pan* is the input to rule B and *pa* is its output.

Stress and Epenthesis in Mohawk

Mohawk is one of the five Northern Iroquoian languages. The present examples are based on the dialect spoken near Montréal. Each set of data illustrates a different aspect of Mohawk phonology. Underlying representations are given on the left, and phonetic forms on the right. Do not be concerned with trying to state the rules accounting for alternations other than those discussed in the questions below.

A. 1. hra+nyahesʌ̃+s   ranahé:zʌ̃s   'he trusts her'

   2. hra+ket+as   ragé:das   'he scrapes'

   3. wa?+hra+ket+?   wahá:gede?   'he scraped'

   4. o+wis+?   ó:wize?   'ice, glass'

   5. wake+nuhwe?+u+ne?   wagenuhwe?ú:ne?   'I had liked it'

   6. ʌ̃+k+hʌ̃te+?   ʌ̃khʌ̃́:de?   'I shall go ahead'

B. 1. ya+k+ni+rʌ̃n+ot+?   yagenirɔ́:node?   'we two (exclusive) are singing'

   2. ya+k+ni+ehyara?+s   yagenehyá:ra?s   'we two (exclusive) remember'

   3. ya+k+wa+rʌ̃n+ot+?   yagwarɔ́:node?   'we (plural exclusive) are singing'

   4. ya+k+wa+ehyara?+s   yagwehyá:ra?s   'we (plural exclusive) remember'

   5. hra+yʌ̃tho+s   rayʌ̃́thos   'he plants'

   6. hra+ehyara?+s   rehyá:ra?s   'he remembers'

   7. ye+k+hrek+s   yékreks   'I push it'

   8. ye+ʌ̃k+hrek+?   yɔ́krege?   'I will push it'

1. In the above forms we notice that a vowel [e] sometimes appears in the final syllable of the phonetic form that does not occur in the underlying representation. State the rule that determines its occurrence.

2. State the Mohawk stress rule.

3. We observe that all vowels are short in underlying representations, but some stressed vowels are long in phonetic representation. Is vowel length predictable? If so, by what rule?

4. The forms in B give evidence of a regular process applying to vowels in sequence. State the rule that describes this process.

C. 1. hra + o + yo?tʌ̃ + c?   royó?de?   'he works'

    2. wa? + hra + o + yo?tʌ̃ + ?   wahoyó?dʌ̃?   'he worked'

    3. hra + kʌ̃ + s   rá:gʌ̃s   'he sees her'

    4. hra + o + kʌ̃   ró:gʌ̃h   'he has seen her'

    5. k + csak + s   gé:zaks   'I look for it'

    6. hra + csak + s   ré:zaks   'he looks for it'

5. What do the forms given in C tell us about the respective ordering of the rules you proposed
    in your answers to problems 2 and 4? Explain your answer.

6. Summarize the rules you have proposed for Mohawk, listing them in the order in which they
    must apply to derive all the above forms correctly. Describe (in step by step fashion) how
    these rules account for the relevant aspects of the form meaning 'I will push it' (see B).
    (Reminder: make sure that your rules account for *all* examples correctly, in particular the
    data of C.)

Indonesian Verb Prefixes

Analyze the following Indonesian words into their constituent morphemes, and work out an underlying representation for each morpheme and each word.

		simple form	prefixed form
1.	'throw'	lempar	m ə lempar
2.	'feel'	rasa	m ə rasa
3.	'represent'	wakil	m ə wakili
4.	'convince'	yakin	m ə yakini
5.	'cook'	masak	m ə masak
6.	'marry'	nikah	m ə nikah
7.	'chat'	ŋaco	m ə ŋaco
8.	'sing'	ɲaɲi	m ə ɲaɲi
9.	'count'	hituŋ	m ə ŋhituŋ
10.	'draw a picture'	gambar	m ə ŋgambar
11.	'send'	kirim	m ə ŋirim
12.	'hear'	d əŋar	m ə nd əŋar
13.	'write'	tulis	m ə nulis
14.	'help'	bantu	m ə mbantu
15.	'hit'	pukul	m ə mukul
16.	'sew'	ǰahit	m əɲǰahit
17.	'note down'	čatat	m əɲčatat
18.	'take'	ambil	m ə ŋambil
19.	'fill up'	isi	m ə ŋisi
20.	'invite'	undaŋ	m ə ŋundaŋ

1. What is the underlying representation of the prefix? Why have you selected this form?

2. State the underlying representations of any other alternating morphemes. Then give the rules that are necessary to derive all observed surface forms.

   Note. The final *i* in the prefixed forms of 3 and 4 may be considered a suffix unique to these two forms.

3. Do any of the rules need to be ordered? Explain your answer.

4. Give the complete underlying representation of the words *m ə mukul* 'hit', *m ə ŋambil* 'take', *m ə masak* 'cook' and *m ə mbantu* 'help'. Then give step-by-step derivations of their surface forms.

Japanese Verb Conjugation

The following forms illustrate verb conjugation in Japanese.

Note. t^s is a voiceless dental affricate.

		present	negative	volitional	past	inchoative	UR
1.	'sleep'	neru	nenai	netai	neta	neyoo	
2.	'see'	miru	minai	mitai	mita	miyoo	
3.	'die'	šinu	šinanai	šinitai	šinda	šinoo	
4.	'read'	yomu	yomanai	yomitai	yonda	yomoo	
5.	'call'	yobu	yobanai	yobitai	yonda	yoboo	
6.	'win'	kat^{s}u	katanai	kačitai	katta	katoo	
7.	'lend'	kasu	kasanai	kašitai	kašita	kasoo	
8.	'boil'	waku	wakanai	wakitai	waita	wakoo	
9.	'pour'	t^{s}ugu	t^{s}uganai	t^{s}ugitai	t^{s}uida	t^{s}ugoo	
10.	'shear'	karu	karanai	karitai	katta	karoo	
11.	'buy'	kau	kawanai	kaitai	katta	kaoo	

1. Determine the underlying representation (UR) of each stem and write it in the space provided. State the underlying representation of each suffix:

2. State the rules accounting for all alternations.

3. Indicate which rules must be ordered, and show (with appropriate examples) why the ordering is crucial in each case.

Abbreviatory Conventions (III)

We sometimes find rules that involve dependencies between two of their terms, to the effect that if a given feature is present in one term, one or more further features must be present in another term. Such rules cannot be expressed by the formal notation developed so far.

Consider, as an example, the alternating sounds [k ~ s], [g ~ ǰ] found in numerous pairs of related words in English:

critical	[k]	criticism	[s]
opaque	[k]	opacity	[s]
analogue	[g]	analogize	[ǰ]
regal	[g]	regicide	[ǰ]

As these forms show, before certain suffixes which we will designate with the feature [+VS], the voiceless velar stop [k] is replaced by [s] and the voiced velar stop [g] is replaced by [ǰ]. What is of interest here is that the two stops are not affected uniformly. While the first becomes an alveolar fricative, the second becomes a palato-alveolar affricate. Thus we see that there is a dependency between a feature of the input (voicing) and two features of the output (anteriority and continuancy).

We may express these dependencies by enclosing the relevant features in subscripted angle brackets, and adding a condition to the rule of the form "a → b" ("a logically implies b", "if a, then b"). The rule of Velar Softening can then be written as follows:

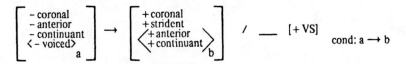

This rule states that a velar stop becomes a strident coronal before any member of the class of [+VS] suffixes, and that, in addition, if the velar is voiceless, the resulting segment is an anterior continuant.

Note that more than one feature may be enclosed in a single pair of brackets, as in the above example. Bracketed features are not restricted to the immediate left and right of the arrow, but may occur in rule environments as well.

Problem 1

In the variety of German spoken in Zürich, Switzerland, there is a regular pattern of vowel alternation (Umlaut) found before a certain class of suffixes, which we may designate by the feature [+U].

$$u: \rightarrow ü:$$
$$u \rightarrow ü$$
$$o: \rightarrow ö:$$
$$o \rightarrow ö$$
$$\mathit{v}: \rightarrow æ:$$
$$\mathit{v} \rightarrow æ$$

State the umlaut rule of this dialect using the angled bracket notation. (Recall that [v:, v] are low back rounded vowels.)

Problem 2

In Kirghiz, we find vowel alternations like the following:

		definite past	past participle
1.	'know'	bildi	bilgen
2.	'give'	berdi	bergen
3.	'laugh'	küldü	külgön
4.	'see'	kördü	körgön
5.	'do'	kɨldɨ	kɨlgan
6.	'take'	aldɨ	algan
7.	'hold'	tuttu	tutkan
8.	'be, become'	boldu	bolgon

1. State the rule accounting for alternations in the feature *back*.

2. State the rule accounting for alternations in the feature *round*, using the angled bracket notation.

Problem 3

In Bamileke (the Feʔfeʔ dialect, as spoken in Petit Diboum), reduplicated syllables always contain one of the high vowels [i ɨ u]. The selection of this vowel is predictable. We find [u] if the first vowel of the next syllable is a high rounded vowel or if it is a nonhigh rounded vowel preceded by a labial or velar consonant. We find [i] if the first vowel of the next syllable is a high unrounded vowel or if it is a nonhigh unrounded vowel preceded by a palatal or alveolar consonant. We find [ɨ] otherwise. Examples are given below.

A.	1.	'carve'	kuu	kukuu
	2.	'kill time'	mo	mumo
	3.	'be afraid'	pɔh	pupɔh
B.	4.	'spoil'	sii	sisii
	5.	'see'	yee	yiyee
	6.	'stand up'	tɛn	titɛn
	7.	'trample'	caʔ	cicaʔ
C.	8.	'punch'	to	tɨto
	9.	'be severe'	cɔh	cɨcɔh
	10.	'hate'	pee	pɨpee
	11.	'go'	ɣɛn	ɣɨɣɛn
	12.	'fry'	kaʔ	kɨkaʔ

Assume the basic form of the reduplicated vowel is [ɨ]. State the rule that accounts for the vowels [u, i]. (Hint: the notation described in "Abbreviatory Conventions II" will be necessary here.)

131

Swahili

The following forms illustrate a regular pattern of singular and plural formation in Swahili.

			singular	plural	UR (stem)
A.	1.	'piece'	ubale	m̩bale	
	2.	'nut-grass'	udago	n̩dago	
	3.	'beer'	ugimbi	ŋgimbi	
	4.	'passage-way'	uǰia	ɲǰia	
	5.	'a bulging'	upaǰa	pʰaǰa, mapaǰa	
	6.	'(type of) knife'	upamba	pʰamba	
	7.	'guardianship'	utunzo	tʰunzo, matunzo	
	8.	'string of beads'	utunda	tʰunda	
	9.	'a cry'	ukelele	kʰelele, makelele	
	10.	'porch'	ukumbi	kʰumbi	
	11.	'a burning'	učoma	čʰoma, mačoma	
	12.	'small intestine'	učaŋgo	čʰaŋgo	
	13.	'imitation'	ufuasi	fuasi, mafuasi	
	14.	'sea-shore'	ufuko	fuko	
	15.	'a ferrying'	uvušo	vušo, mavušo	
	16.	'speck of dust'	uvumbi	vumbi	
	17.	'night'	usiku	siku, masiku	
	18.	'(type of) powder'	usira	sira	
	19.	'sewing'	ušono	šono, mašono	
	20.	'bead'	ušaŋga	šaŋga	
	21.	'sky, heaven'	uwiŋgu	m̩biŋgu	
	22.	'duality'	uwili	m̩bili	
	23.	'tongue'	ulimi	n̩dimi	
	24.	'length, distance'	urefu	n̩defu	
	25.	'throat'	umio	mio	
	26.	'song'	wimbo	ɲimbo	
	27.	'razor'	wembe	ɲembe	
	28.	'time'	wakati	ɲakati	
	29.	'eyebrow'	uši	ɲuši	

B.	Additional data, illustrating another pattern of singular and plural formation:			
	30.	'axe'	šoka	mašoka
	31.	'fruit'	tunda	matunda
	32.	'safe'	kaša	makaša

1. Consider the nouns illustrated in part A. What is the underlying form of the singular prefix? What rule determines its pattern of alternation?

2. Consider the following choices for the underlying representation of the plural prefix in part A: /n-/; /ɲ-/; Ø. Which choice can be defended on the basis of the simplicity of the description and the naturalness of the rule(s) required to describe the alternations?

3. State the simplest set of rules required to account for all surface forms, and determine the order in which they apply.

4. Give derivations for 'piece', 'string of beads', 'sea-shore', and 'tongue' in the singular and plural (8 forms in all).

Turkish Nouns

The following lists give representative noun forms in Turkish.

Notes. nom: nominative, poss: possessed, acc: accusative, dat: dative, abl: ablative, pl: plural

/k, g/ are palatalized before front vowels; these variants are not marked in the transcriptions.

		nom.	poss.	dat.	abl.	nom. pl.	poss./acc. pl.
1.	'room'	oda	odası	odaya	odadan	odalar	odaları
2.	'river'	dere	deresi	dereye	dereden	derel^yer	derel^yeri
3.	'fox'	til^yki	til^ykisi	til^ykiye	til^ykiden	til^ykil^yer	til^ykil^yleri
4.	'press iron'	ütü	ütüsü	ütüye	ütüden	ütül^yer	ütül^yeri
5.	'bee'	arı	arısı	arıya	arıdan	arılar	arıları
6.	'pipe'	boru	borusu	boruya	borudan	borular	boruları
7.	'cap'	kep	kepi	kepe	kepten	kepl^yer	kepl^yeri
8.	'horse'	at	atı	ata	attan	atlar	atları
9.	'worm'	kurt	kurdu	kurda	kurttan	kurtlar	kurtları
10.	'hair'	sač	sačı	sača	sačtan	sačlar	sačları
11.	'steep'	sarp	sarpı	sarpa	sarptan	sarplar	sarpları
12.	'end'	son	sonu	sona	sondan	sonlar	sonları
13.	'village'	köy	köyü	köye	köyden	köyl^yer	köyl^yeri
14.	'power'	güč	güǰü	güǰe	güčten	güčl^yer	güčl^yeri
15.	'stalk'	sap	sapı	sapa	saptan	saplar	sapları
16.	'bottom'	alt	altı	alta	alttan	altlar	altları
17.	'color'	renk	rengi	renge	renkten	renkl^yer	renkl^yeri
18.	'ball'	balo	balosu	baloya	balodan	balolar	baloları
19.	'container'	kap	kabı	kaba	kaptan	kaplar	kapları
20.	'taste'	tat	tadı	tada	tattan	tatlar	tatları
21.	'Ahmed'	ahmet	ahmedi	ahmede	ahmetten	ahmetl^yer	ahmetl^yeri
22.	'young'	genč	genǰi	genǰe	genčten	genčl^yer	genčl^yeri
23.	'foot'	ayak	ayaı	ayaa	ayaktan	ayaklar	ayakları
24.	'cow'	inek	inei	inee	inekten	inekl^yer	inekl^yeri
25.	'law school'	hukuk	hukuu	hukua	hukuktan	hukuklar	hukukları
26.	'profession'	mesl^yek	mesl^yei	mesl^yee	mesl^yekten	mesl^yekl^yer	mesl^yekl^yeri
27.	'rent'	kira:	kira:sı	kira:ya	kira:dan	kira:lar	kira:ları
28.	'past'	ma:zi:	ma:zi:si	ma:zi:ye	ma:zi:den	ma:zi:l^yer	ma:zi:l^yeri
29.	'curiosity'	merak	mera:kı	mera:ka	meraktan	meraklar	merakları
30.	'law'	hukuk	huku:ku	huku:ka	hukuktan	hukuklar	hukukları

31.	'good deed'	sevap	seva:bɨ	seva:ba	sevaptan	sevaplar	sevaplarɨ
32.	'method'	usulʸ	usu:lʸü	usu:lʸe	usulʸden	usulʸlʸer	usulʸlʸeri
33.	'heart'	kalʸp	kalʸbi	kalʸbe	kalʸpten	kalʸplʸer	kalʸplʸeri
34.	'watch'	saat	saati	saate	saatten	saatlʸer	saatlʸeri

1. Identify the alternants of the following suffixes:

   a. possessed:

   b. dative:

   c. ablative:

   d. plural:

2. List the alternants of the following noun stems:

   a. 'cap'

   b. 'horse'

   c. 'worm'

   d. 'color'

   e. 'Ahmed'

   f. 'law school'

   g. 'law'

   h. 'rent'

3. Consider the following four hypotheses:

   The underlying form of Turkish noun stems is always
   identical to the surface form of:

   a. the nominative stem

   b. the possessed stem

   c. the ablative stem

   d. none of the above

   Which hypothesis is most likely to be correct on the basis of the present data? Argue for your decision by showing that alternative solutions lead to more complicated descriptions.

4. State the rules that account for the variant forms of the noun stems.

5. State the rule(s) that determine the variant forms of suffixes. (It should not be necessary to mention specific suffixes in your statement.)

The Creole Language Spoken in São Tomé

The data given below illustrate some of the major correspondences between Portuguese and the creole language spoken in São Tomé (ST), an island off the coast of Africa. Examine the related Portuguese and ST forms and determine the linguistic rules that most succinctly describe the relationship. Work this out separately on a sheet of scratch paper. Can one predict the ST forms from the Portuguese forms? Can one predict the Portuguese forms from the ST forms? Determine which language provides the better point of departure.

Note. The phonemes /č, ǰ/ do not occur in Portuguese.

	P	ST	
1.	vešpʌ	vešpa	'wasp'
2.	šigar	šiga	'to arrive'
3.	sɛgu	sɛgu	'blind'
4.	šumbu	sumbu	'lead'
5.	pɜškar	piška	'to fish'
6.	řatu	latu	'rat'
7.	artɜ	ači	'art'
8.	tašu	tasu	'pan'
9.	kulpʌ	klupa	'blame'
10.	řɜšpʌitu	lišpetu	'courtesy'
11.	ʌguʎʌ	guya	'needle'
12.	tirar	čila	'to take out'
13.	dyabu	ǰabu	'devil'
14.	šʌmar	sama	'to call'
15.	kwazɜ	kwaži	'almost'
16.	tardɜ	taǰi	'afternoon'
17.	idadɜ	daǰi	'age'
18.	kʌprišu	kaplisu	'caprice'
19.	fɛřu	fɛlu	'iron'
20.	brõzɜ	blõži	'bronze'
21.	fižir	fiži	'to pretend'
22.	žemʌ	zema	'egg yolk'
23.	diʌ	ǰa	'day'
24.	forsa	fosa	'strength'
25.	mɔrtɜ	mɔči	'death'
26.	pulgʌ	pluga	'flea'
27.	bišu	bisu	'animal'

28.	pɜdir	piǰi	'to ask'
29.	tiʌ	ča	'aunt'
30.	kʌižu	kezu	'cheese'
31.	pʌlasyu	palašu	'palace'
32.	bʌrbʌiru	blabelu	'barber'
33.	ifɛr̄nu	fɛnu	'hell'
34.	sinku	šinku	'five'

1. State all the rules of correspondence between Portuguese and ST, giving examples of each one. Should any of your rules be ordered? Explain how your rules account for the pronunciations of 'devil', 'bronze', and 'barber'.

2. In the data we see the following correspondences:

P	:	ST
s		š
š		s
š		š
s		s

Is this a sporadic, random pattern of correspondence, or is it a predictable one? Explain your answer.

Klamath Prefixes

Klamath has prefixation processes that form various inflected senses of the verb, including "distributive" (plural subject), reflexive-reciprocal, and causative senses. Representative forms are given below.

Data A.

1.	hi:wi	'hauls'	sihi:wi	'haul each other'
2.	m'a:s?a	'is sick'	m'am'a:s?a	'are sick'
			həsm'a:s?a	'makes sick'
3.	pe:wa	'bathes'	pepe:wa	'bathe'
			hespe:wa	'causes to bathe'
4.	sti:q'a	'cramps'	stisti:q'a	'cramp'
5.	Ge:ǰiga	'is tired'	GeGe:ǰiga	'are tired'
			sneGe:ǰiga	'makes tired'
6.	smo:l'a	'smokes a hide'	smosmo:l'a	'smoke a hide'
			hosmo:l'a	'causes someone to smoke a hide'
7.	twa:q'a	'smears'	sətwa:q'a	'smears oneself'
8.	lme:lGa	'(pl objects) sink'	snelme:lGa	'causes pl. objects to sink'

1. Identify the four prefixes illustrated in this data, stating the rules that account for the variation in their shape.

Data B.

1.	čipale:?a	'tattoos'	sičpale:?a	'has oneself tattooed'
2.	paga	'barks'	pəpga	'bark'
			snəpga	'makes bark'
3.	lmoya	'feels passionate'	lmolmya	'feel passionate'
4.	nt'op'a	'sours'	nt'ontp'a	'sour'
			snontp'a	'causes something to sour'
5.	sn'oGa	'catches'	sn'osnGa	'catch'
6.	l?ega	'is drunk'	l?elga	'are drunk'
7.	s?ina	'has coitus'	s?is?a	'have coitus'
8.	swina	'sings'	hiswa	'makes someone sing'
			swiswa	'sing'
9.	swapətta	'ties to'	swaso:pətta	'tie to'
10.	sl'ow'iwy'a	'trots'	hoslw'iwy'a	'makes trot'
11.	nkililk'a	'is dusty'	sninklilk'a	'makes dusty'
12.	s?awi:ga	'is angry'	s?əswi:ga	'are angry'

Data C.

1.	čonwa	'vomits'	hosčənwa	'makes vomit'
			čočənwa	'vomit'
2.	sipča	'puts out a fire'	sisəpča	'put out a fire'
3.	Gəttk'a	'is cold'	GaGəttk'a	'are cold'
			snaGəttk'a	'makes cold'
4.	domna	'hears'	dodəmna	'hear'
			sodəmna	'hear each other'
5.	swəqča	'cries'	swəswəqča	'cry'
			həswəqča	'makes someone cry'
6.	p'etq'a	'blinks once'	snep'ətq'a	'makes someone blink'
7.	č'ol?a	'has a cramp'	č'oč'əl?a	'have cramps'
8.	kičw'a	'pokes in the eye'	sikəčw'a	'pokes oneself, each other in the eye'
9.	siwga	'fights'	siso:ga	'fight'
10.	pe:wa	'bathes'	hehəspe:wa	'cause to bathe'
11.	dɔqča	'scratches'	səsdɔqča	'scratch themselves, each other'
12.	wipga	'escapes'	snisnwəpgis	'rescuer'

2. Is [ə] an underlying phoneme?   Explain your answer.

3. Assign a unique underlying form to each of the verb roots illustrated in the above data. State the rules that relate these underlying forms to the surface alternants. Determine whether any of your rules must be ordered.

4. Show how your rules account for the alternations in the following forms:

- a. 'causes something to sour'
- b. 'are drunk'
- c. 'makes dusty'
- d. 'hear each other'
- e. 'cause to bathe'
- f. 'rescuer'

Russian Nominal Declension

Establish the underlying representation of the stems and case endings in the paradigms below. Work out the alternations in vowel quality that depend on the word accent and on palatalization and state the ordered rules.

Notes. [ɨ] = [+ high, – low, + back, – round]   [o] = [+ low, – high, + back, + round]
      [ɛ] = [+ low, – high, – back, – round]   [e] = [– low, – high, – back, – round]

			nom. sg.	gen. pl.	dat. sg.	nom. pl.
A.	1.	'moon'	luná	lún	lun^{y}ɛ́	lúnɨ
	2.	'hole'	dɨrá	dɨr	dɨr^{y}ɛ́	dɨrɨ
	3.	'grass'	travá	tráf	trav^{y}ɛ́	trávɨ
	4.	'saw'	p^{y}ilá	p^{y}íl	p^{y}il^{y}ɛ́	p^{y}ílɨ
	5.	'wave'	valná	vóln	valn^{y}ɛ́	vólnɨ
	6.	'head'	galavá	galóf	galav^{y}ɛ́	gólavɨ
	7.	'gland'	žɨl^{y}izá	žɨl^{y}ós	žɨl^{y}iz^{y}ɛ́	žél^{y}izɨ
	8.	'wife'	žɨná	žón	žɨn^{y}ɛ́	žónɨ
	9.	'snake'	zm^{y}iyá	zm^{y}éy	zm^{y}iyɛ́	zm^{y}éyi
	10.	'change'	m^{y}ɛ́na	m^{y}ɛ́n	m^{y}én^{y}i	m^{y}ɛ́nɨ
	11.	'shroud'	p^{y}il^{y}iná	p^{y}il^{y}ón	p^{y}il^{y}in^{y}ɛ́	p^{y}il^{y}inɨ
	12.	'conversation'	b^{y}is^{y}ɛ́da	b^{y}is^{y}ɛ́t	b^{y}is^{y}éd^{y}i	b^{y}is^{y}ɛ́dɨ
	13.	'sorrow'	b^{y}idá	b^{y}ét	b^{y}id^{y}ɛ́	b^{y}édɨ
	14.	'heel'	p^{y}itá	p^{y}át	p^{y}it^{y}ɛ́	p^{y}itɨ
	15.	'wall'	st^{y}iná	st^{y}ɛ́n	st^{y}in^{y}ɛ́	st^{y}ɛ́nɨ

B.   Additional data: the behavior of velars

		nom. sg.	gen. pl.	dat. sg.	nom. pl.
1.	'river'	r^{y}iká	r^{y}ék	r^{y}ik^{y}ɛ́	r^{y}ék^{y}i
2.	'servant'	slugá	slúk	slug^{y}ɛ́	slúg^{y}i
3.	'flea'	blaxá	blóx	blax^{y}ɛ́	blóx^{y}i

C.   Additional data: prepositions (and behavior of velars)

1. itál^{y}iyu 'Italy' (acc.)   v ɨtál^{y}iyu 'to Italy'   cf. v^{y}itál^{y}iyu 'Vitaly' (name—dat. sg.)

2. íru 'Ira' (acc. sg.)   k ɨr^{y}i 'to Ira'   cf. k^{y}ír^{y}i 'Kyra' (name—dat. sg.)

3. ɛ́tamu 'this' (dat. sg.)   k ɛ́tamu 'to this'   cf. k^{y}ɛ́tam 'Kets' (name of tribe—dat. pl.)

Another Children's Language

At age two years, two months, S, a lively and intelligent child, was producing one-word utterances and short sentences. His English father, a trained phonetician, noted down his single-word utterances at frequent but irregular intervals. At this stage in the development of his language, S had a consistent pronunciation for each word in his vocabulary. Examples of these words are given in the following list. The adult word is given at the left, and S's pronunciation at the right. Where the adult pronunciation differed from common American pronunciations it is given in brackets.

1.	sock	gɔk	18.	table	be:bu
2.	leg	gɛk	19.	bus	bʌt
3.	singing	giŋiŋ	20.	John	dɔn
4.	chockie	gɔgi:	21.	bump	bʌp
5.	stop	bɔp	22.	drink	gik
6.	spoon	bu:n	23.	skin	gin
7.	zoo	du:	24.	stuck	gʌk
8.	other [ʌ̌ðə]	ʌdə	25.	nipple	mibu
9.	scream	gi:m	26.	Smith	mit
10.	uncle	ʌgu	27.	brush	bʌt
11.	dark [da:k]	ga:k	28.	bath [ba:θ]	ba:t
12.	lock	gɔk	29.	tent	dɛt
13.	snake	ŋe:k	30.	thank you	gɛgu
14.	knife	maip	31.	tickle	gigu
15.	new [nyu:]	nu:	32.	crumb	gʌm
16.	apple	ɛbu	33.	angry [æŋgri:]	ɛŋi
17.	play	be:	34.	swing	wiŋ

1. Transcribe the first seven words of the left-hand column in broad phonetic transcription the way they would be pronounced in most American dialects.

2. State the rules needed to derive S's forms from the adult's forms, for consonants only. (Do not be concerned with the child's rendering of vowels and diphthongs.) Your rules should be given in a single ordered list, so that the child's forms can be derived from the adult forms by applying all relevant rules one after another in the order given.

3. Determine all cases in which one rule is *crucially* ordered before or after another rule. Explain why this ordering is necessary, mentioning specific examples.

4. Show how your rules apply to the adult form to account for S's pronunciation of the following: leg, chockie, stop, drink, brush, angry.

Yokuts

Data A

	aorist passive	aorist	future passive	
1.	xatit	xathin	xatnit	'eat'
2.	gopit	gophin	gopnit	'take care of an infant'
3.	giyit	giyhin	giynit	'touch'
4.	mutut	muthun	mutnut	'swear'
5.	sa:pit	saphin	sapnit	'burn'
6.	go:bit	gobhin	gobnit	'take in'
7.	me:kit	mekhin	meknit	'swallow'
8.	?o:tut	?othun	?otnut	'steal'
9.	panat	pana:hin	pana:nit	'arrive'
10.	hoyot	hoyo:hin	hoyo:nit	'name'
11.	?ilet	?ile:hin	?ile:nit	'fan'
12.	cuyot	cuyo:hun	cuyo:nut	'urinate'
13.	paxa:tit	paxathin	paxatnit	'mourn'
14.	?opo:tit	?opothin	?opotnit	'arise from bed'
15.	hibe:yit	hibeyhin	hibeynit	'bring water'
16.	sudo:kut	sudokhun	sudoknut	'remove'

1. Find the environment in which a long vowel can appear. When an alternation of short and long vowels is observable, which one is to be considered more basic?

2. Determine the underlying vowel system by considering the underlying form of each verb.

3. Give the underlying form of each suffix. Try to find the rule to generate alternants. (Do not formulate the rule here.)

Data B

	dubitative	gerund	imperative	
1.	paʔtal	paʔittaw	paʔitka	'fight'
2.	logwol	logiwtaw	logiwka	'pulverize'
3.	ʔilkal	ʔiliktaw	ʔilikka	'sing'
4.	hubsal	hubustaw	hubuska	'choose'
5.	ʔamlal	ʔa:miltaw	ʔa:milka	'help'
6.	moxlol	mo:xiltaw	mo:xilka	'grow old'
7.	sental	se:nittaw	se:nitka	'smell'
8.	wowlal	wo:wultaw	wo:wulka	'stand up'

Data C

In the following are given the consequent gerundial and imperative forms of some of the verbs given in Data A.

	consequent gerundial		imperative
1.	giymi	5.	xatka
2.	ʔotmu	6.	gobko
3.	panam	7.	ʔilek
4.	ʔopotmi	8.	sudokka

4. a. Give the underlying forms of verbs in Data B.
   b. Give the underlying form of suffixes in Data B and Data C.
   c. Give the expected form of the aorist and aorist passive of the verbs in Data B.

5. Give the ordered set of rules to generate all forms given above from the underlying representations you have set up.

Rules that Affect more than one Segment

Many languages make use of rules affecting more than one segment at once. The most common of these are rules of metathesis where in a particular context, a sequence elsewhere appearing as AB appears instead as BA.

A simple example of this is provided by the Lithuanian conjugation, where a coronal continuant [s z š ž] is permuted with a following velar stop [k g] before a consonant-initial suffix.

	3. pres.	3. past	infinitive	imp. pl.
'tear'	drɛ:skʸa	dre:ske:	dre:ksti	dre:kskite
'knit'	mɛ:zga	me:zge:	mɛgsti	mɛgskite
'toss'	blɔ:škʸa	blɔ:ške:	blɔ:kšti	blɔ:kškite

Formally, such processes are characterized with the help of transformational rules of the following form (where X or Y may be null):

SD: X   A   B   Y   SC: 1   3   2   4
      1   2   3   4

The Lithuanian forms above are then described by means of the rule:

$$
\text{SD:} \quad
\begin{bmatrix} - \text{sonorant} \\ + \text{continuant} \\ + \text{coronal} \end{bmatrix}
\begin{bmatrix} - \text{sonorant} \\ - \text{coronal} \\ - \text{anterior} \end{bmatrix}
[- \text{syllabic}]
$$

$$
\qquad\qquad 1 \qquad\qquad 2 \qquad\qquad 3
$$

$$
\text{SC:} \qquad 2 \qquad\qquad 1 \qquad\qquad 3
$$

Latvian Nominal Declension

A. Assume that you have three masculine and three feminine declensions as shown:

I. Masculine

	'father'	'swan'	'market'
sg. nom.	tæ:vs	gulbis	tirgus
loc.	tæ:va:	gulbi:	tirgu:
acc.	tæ:vu	gulbi	tirgu
dat.	tæ:vam	gulbim	tirgum
gen.	tæ:va	gulbya	tirgus
pl. nom.	tæ:vi	gulbyi	tirgi
loc.	tæ:vuɔs	gulbyuɔs	tirguɔs
acc.	tæ:vus	gulbyus	tirgus
dat.	tæ:viæm	gulbyiæm	tirgiæm
gen.	tæ:vu	gulbyu	tirgu

II. Feminine

	'sister'	'land, earth'	'cow'
sg. nom.	ma:sa	zeme	guɔvs
loc.	ma:sa:	zeme:	guɔvi:
acc.	ma:su	zemi	guɔvi
dat.	ma:say	zemey	guɔviy
gen.	ma:sas	zemes	guɔvs
pl. nom.	ma:sas	zemes	guɔvis
loc.	ma:sa:s	zeme:s	guɔvi:s
acc.	ma:sas	zemes	guɔvis
dat.	ma:sa:m	zeme:m	guɔvi:m
gen.	ma:su	zemyu	guɔvyu

1. Determine the underlying representation of each form, indicating morpheme divisions.

2. State the rules deriving the surface forms from the underlying forms.

B. Indefinite and definite adjectives have separate declensions. These are given below for the root *lab*- 'good'.

	m. indef.	fem. indef.	m. def.	fem. def.
sg. nom.	labs	laba	labays	laba:
loc.	laba:	laba:	labaya:	labaya:
acc.	labu	labu	labuɔ	labuɔ
dat.	labam	labay	labayam	labayay
gen.	laba	labas	laba:	laba:s
pl. nom.	labi	labas	labiæ	laba:s
loc.	labuɔs	laba:s	labayuɔs	labaya:s
acc.	labus	labas	labuɔs	laba:s
dat.	labiæm	laba:m	labayiæm	labaya:m
gen.	labu	labu	labuɔ	labuɔ

3. Assuming that some or all of the rules stated in your answer to part 2 of this problem may be operative in the adjectival declension, show that all forms in the above paradigms can be described by phonologically conditioned rules alone.

Icelandic Conjugation

The following forms illustrate infinitive and past tense formation in Icelandic.

Note. [ɼ] and [ɬ] are velarized [r], [l] respectively.

		infinitive	past tense	UR (stem)
1.	'lock'	lai:sa	laistɪ	
2.	'show'	si:na	sintɪ	
3.	'measure'	mai:la	mailtɪ	
4.	'move'	fai:ra	fairðɪ	
5.	'wake'	va:kʰa	vaxtɪ	
6.	'stare'	klau:pʰa	klauftɪ	
7.	'utilize'	ni:tʰa	nihtɪ	
8.	'lay eggs'	vɛrpa	vɛr̥tɪ	
9.	'stay overnight'	cɪsta	cɪstɪ	
10.	'lick'	lɛ:pʰya	laftɪ	
11.	'cover'	hɪlya	høltɪ	
12.	'put'	sɛ:tʰya	sɛhtɪ	
13.	'wake up'	vɛ:cʰa	vaxtɪ	
14.	'cover'	θɛ:cʰa	θaxtɪ	
15.	'clear the throat'	raisca	raistɪ	
16.	'ring'	hrɪɲca	hrɪŋtɪ	
17.	'tease'	ɛrca	ɛɼðɪ	
18.	'follow'	fɪlca	fɪɬtɪ	
19.	'bless'	sɪkna	sɪŋtɪ	
20.	'frown'	ɪkla	ɪɬtɪ	

1. Is vowel length predictable in Icelandic? If not, present minimal (or near-minimal) pairs showing contrastive vowel length. If so, state the rule accounting for vowel length.

2. The infinitives in examples (10)—(20) are formed with a suffix not used in forming the other examples. What is the most likely underlying form of this suffix?

3. Do [cʰ] and [c] occur in underlying representations? Why or why not?

4. Work out underlying representations for all verb stems and enter them in the space provided. Then state the rules accounting for all consonant alternations (vowel alternations may be ignored). Give derivations of 'clear the throat', 'ring', 'follow', and 'bless' in both the infinitive and the past tense (8 forms in all).

Okpe Conjugation

The following forms illustrate vowel alternations in Okpe. Nasality, which is distinctive in this language, is not indicated in our examples.

			imperative	3 sg. past	2 sg. past	infinitive	1 pl. incl. contin.	UR (stem)
A.	1.	'pull'	ti	o tiri	wi tiri	etyo	e tyɛ	
	2.	'do'	ru	o ruru	wi ruru	ɛrwo	e rwɛ	
	3.	'bury'	si	o siri	wi siri	esyo	e syɛ	
	4.	'fan'	zu	o zuru	wi zuru	ezwo	e zwɛ	
B.	5.	'buy'	dɛ	ɔ dɛre	we dɛre	ɛdɛ	a dɛ	
	6.	'drink'	da	ɔ dare	we dare	ɛda	a da	
	7.	'dig'	tɔ	ɔ tɔre	we tɔre	ɛtɔ	a tɔ	
	8.	'run'	zɛ	ɔ zɛre	we zɛre	ɛzɛ	a zɛ	
C.	9.	'fill'	se	o seri	wi seri	ese	e se	
	10.	'steal'	so	o sori	wi sori	eso	e so	
	11.	'defecate'	ne	o neri	wi neri	ene	e ne	
	12.	'rot'	gbo	o gbori	wi gbori	egbo	e gbo	
D.	13.	'eat'	re	ɔ rere	we rere	ɛryɔ	a rya	
	14.	'sing'	so	ɔ soro	we soro	ɛswɔ	a swa	
	15.	'refuse'	te	ɔ tere	we tere	ɛtyɔ	a tya	
	16.	'come'	rhe	ɔ rhere	we rhere	ɛrhyɔ	a rhya	

E. Additional data: Further forms of the continuative include:

    o tyɛ (3. sg.), wi tyɛ (2. sg.), etc.

1. Determine a unique underlying representation for each stem represented in the above data and write it in the space provided. State the underlying representation of each affix below:

2. Should glides be considered underlying or can they all be derived by rule? Explain your answer.

3. State the rules required to derive all surface forms from all underlying forms. Provide sample derivations illustrating your rules. Do any of your rules require morphological conditioning?

165

Noun Declension in Ancient and Modern Greek

Given below are forms from a selection of noun paradigms, Ancient Greek (AG) on the left and Modern Greek (MG) on the right.

Note. V̂ indicates the circumflex accent, V́ the acute accent.

sg:	singular	masc: masculine gender
pl:	plural	fem: feminine gender
nom:	nominative case	neut: neuter gender
gen:	genitive case	
acc:	accusative case	

		'father' (masc.)		'crow' (masc.)		'citizen' (masc.)	
sg.	nom.	paté:r	patéras	kóraks	kórakas	políte:s	polítis
	gen.	patrós	patéra	kórakos	kóraka	polítu:	políti
	acc.	patéra	patéra	kóraka	kóraka	políte:n	políti
pl.	gen.	patéro:n	patéro	koráko:n	koráko	políto:n	políto

		'brother' (masc.)		'mother' (fem.)		'woman' (fem.)	
sg.	nom.	adelpʰós	aðelfós	mé:te:r	mitéra	güné:	γinéka
	gen.	adelpʰû:	aðelfú	mé:tros	mitéras	günaîkos	γinékas
	acc.	adelpʰón	aðelfó	me:téra	mitéra	günaîka	γinéka
pl.	gen.	adelpʰô:n	aðelfó	me:téro:n	mitéro	günaíko:n	γinéko

		'hope' (fem.)		'judgement' (fem.)		'sister' (fem.)	
sg.	nom.	elpís	elpíða	krísis	krísi	adelpʰé:	aðelfí
	gen.	elpídos	elpíðas	kríseo:s	krísis	adelpʰé:s	aðelfís
	acc.	elpída	elpíða	krísin	krísi	adelpʰé:n	aðelfí
pl.	gen.	elpído:n	elpíðo	kríseo:n	kríso	adelpʰô:n	aðelfó

		'door' (fem.)		'face' (neut.)		'name' (neut.)	
sg.	nom.	tʰǘra:	θíra	próso:pon	prósopo	ónoma	ónoma
	gen.	tʰǘra:s	θíras	prosó:pu:	prosópu	onómatos	onómatos
	acc.	tʰǘra:n	θíra	próso:pon	prósopo	ónoma	ónoma
pl.	gen.	tʰǘro:n	θíro	prosó:po:n	prosópo	onomáto:n	onomáto

1. Describe the changes which have affected the Greek phonological system. Take into account the following:

    (a) synchronic rules operating in AG and those operating in MG;
    (b) comparison of the two sets of rules.

    To what extent can the changes displayed in the data be attributed to changes in rule systems, and to what extent should they be attributed to restructuring (replacement of one underlying form by another)? Discuss, as appropriate, such factors as rule simplification, rule loss, rule reordering, transparency/opacity.

2. Can the changes in the system of nominal inflection be attributed entirely to phonological factors of the sort listed in question 1? If not, what other factors must be taken into account?

6. Prosodic Phonology

Noun Compounding in English

Compound nouns in English may be made up of two simple nouns:

radio station

building council

pretzel seller

evening class

In these two-member compounds, the main stress falls on the first word, as indicated by the underlining. Longer noun compounds may differ in their immediate constituent (IC) analysis. For example:

[radio station] manager	'manager of a radio station'
evening [computer class]	'computer class held in the evening'

These differences in constituent structure may correspond to differences in the location of the main stress, as the examples indicate.

1. In the following exercise you are asked to determine the IC analysis of a selection of longer compounds. First determine how many (plausible!) meanings each compound has. For each meaning, indicate the IC analysis with brackets and write a paraphrase as has been done above. Finally, underline the word that bears the main stress (as indicated by higher pitch, longer duration, or greater loudness). If you are not a native speaker of English you should find a native speaker to serve as informant. An example is given below:

   glass flower case

[glass flower] case	'a case for glass flowers'
glass [flower case]	'a flower case made of glass'

   Notice that the IC(s) you have selected should form units of sense similar to the meaning they have in the compound as a whole. For example, if we had mistakenly analyzed *evening computer class* as [evening computer] class, the IC *evening computer* would mean something very different from what it means in the compound.

1.	garbage can collector	7.	auto industry disaster relief
2.	supermarket delivery service	8.	hand gun control lobby
3.	housing department employee	9.	park department land survey
4.	metal working tools	10.	law school language requirement changes
5.	opera company ticket office	11.	police captain association philosophy colloquium
6.	pretzel seller scandal report	12.	auto polish can label collector admirer

2. Formulate the rule that determines which word bears the main stress in English compounds on the basis of your answers to question 1.

Arabic Broken Plurals

The following forms illustrate a productive system of plural formation in Classical Arabic.

Notes. Ç = emphatic consonant, ḥ = [ħ].

	singular	plural	
1.	ǰundab	ǰanaadib	'locust'
2.	šayṭaan	šayaaṭiin	'devil'
3.	sulṭaan	salaaṭiin	'sultan'
4.	šuʔbuub	šaʔaabiib	'shower of rain'
5.	nuwwaar	nawaawiir	'white flowers'
6.	maktab	makaatib	'office'
7.	miftaaḥ	mafaatiiḥ	'key'
8.	ʕankabuut	ʕanaakib	'spider'
9.	ǰaḥmariš	ǰaḥaamir	'lazy old woman'
10.	safarǰal	safaariǰ	'quince'
11.	ʕandaliib	ʕanaadil	'nightingale'
12.	namuuðaǰ	namaaðiǰ	'type'
13.	zalzalat	zalaazil	'earthquake'
14.	ǰudǰud	ǰadaaǰid	'cricket'
15.	ziʕnifat	zaʕaanif	'fin of a fish'
16.	fuqqaaʕat	faqaaqiiʕ	'bubble'
17.	xaatam	xawaatim	'signet ring'
18.	baaʕiθ	bawaaʕiθ	'motive'
19.	ṣaaʕiqat	ṣawaaʕiq	'thunderbolt'
20.	ǰaamuus	ǰawaamiis	'buffalo'
21.	qaanuun	qawaaniin	'canon (of law)'

1. Determine the generalizations that hold of the plural nouns as a whole.

2. Is the relationship between the singular and plural form of each noun totally arbitrary? If not, state all the regularities that you can find.

3. What is the plural "affix"? How can this be described in terms of autosegmental representation?

Ogori Contraction

The following examples illustrate vowel and tone contraction in Ogori (Nigeria). Tones are indicated as follows:

à = low tone

a = mid tone (unmarked)

á = high tone

A.   Noun + adjective combinations

1.	ìgìlà	'yam'	òkeke	'small'	ìgìlòkeke	'small yam'
2.	ɔtɛ́lɛ́	'pot'	ɔkɛ̌ka	'big'	ɔtɛ́lɔkɛ̌ka	'big pot'
3.	ɛsá	'cloth'	ɔrírĩ	'black'	ɛsɔrírĩ	'black pot'
4.	úbó	'house'	óbòrò	'good'	úbóbòrò	'good house'
5.	ébí	'water'	óbòrò	'good'	ébóbòrò	'good water'
6.	ìǰá	'woman'	òsúdá	'old'	ìǰósúdá	'old woman'
7.	ɔbèlè	'mat'	ɔnɛ	'this'	ɔbèlɔnɛ	'this mat'
8.	ɔdɔ	'rat'	ɔnɛ	'this'	ɔdɔnɛ	'this rat'
9.	úwó	'dog'	ɔnɛbɛ	'that'	úwɔnɛbɛ	'that dog'
10.	ɔbèlè	'mat'	óbòrò	'good'	ɔ̀bèlóbòrò	'good mat'

B.   Numeral + numeral combinations

11.	èbɔrɛ̀	'two'	ɛ̀bɔrɛ̀bɔrɛ̀	'two by two'
12.	ufɔ́mbɔrɛ	'seven'	ufɔ́mbɔrufɔ́mbɔrɛ	'seven by seven'

1.   State the rules accounting for the data above.

2.   Consider the following two hypotheses:

    A.   Tones are segmental features of vowels on a par with such features as 'high' or 'continuant'.

    B.   Tones are autosegmental.

Indicate whether the above data allows us to choose between these two hypotheses.

Mende Suffixes

The following data illustrate three suffixes in Mende (Sierra Leone). Unsuffixed stems are given on the left. Tones are indicated as follows:

á = high

à = low

â = falling

ǎ = rising

'á = high preceded by downstep

		'on'	indef. plural	def. singular	
1.	kɔ	kɔmá	kɔ ngà:	kɔí	'war'
2.	pélé	pélémá	pélèngà:	péléí	'house'
3.	mbû	mbúmà	mbúngà:	mbú'í	'owl'
4.	ngílà	ngílàmà	ngílàngà:	ngíl'éí	'dog'
5.	mbǎ	mbàmá	mbǎngà:	mbèí	'rice'
6.	bèlè	bèlèmá	bèlèngà:	bèlèí	'trousers'
7.	nyàhâ	nyàhámà	nyàhángà:	nyàhé'í	'woman'
8.	nàvó	nàvómá	nàvóngà:	nàvóí	'money'
9.	fândé	fàndèmá	fàndéngà:	fàndèí	'cotton'

1. Propose an underlying representation for each of the suffixes.

2. State the underlying tone melody of each noun.

3. State the rules accounting for all tonal alternations. (Vowel alternations may be ignored.)

Southern Paiute Stress

The nonsense forms below illustrate the stress distribution in Southern Paiute words as well as a number of other phonological processes which in various ways depend on stress.

Notes. Capital A represents a voiceless vowel, á, a vowel with primary stress, and à, a vowel with secondary stress.

1.	páẉA	9.	mawáẉA	17.	m̥ApáẉA
2.	pawáA	10.	mawáwàA	18.	m̥ApáwàA
3.	paáẉA	11.	mawáàẉA	19.	m̥ApáàẉA
4.	paáwàA	12.	**mawáawàA**	20.	m̥ApáawàA
5.	páppA	13.	mawáppA	21.	m̥ApáppA
6.	pApáA	14.	mawáppàA	22.	m̥ApáppàA
7.	paáppA	15.	mawáàppA	23.	m̥ApáàppA
8.	paáppàA	16.	mawáApàA	24.	m̥ApáApàA

1. State in words first the rule governing the distribution of secondary stress, then the rule for primary stress.

2. Give a formal statement in metrical terms of the Southern Paiute stress rule.

3. Assuming that all glides in the above example derive from stops, state the context in which stops become glides ([p] → [w]). (Hint: stops that do not become glides in this context are underlying geminates.)

4. State the context in which vowels are devoiced.

5. State the context in which sonorant consonants become voiceless.

6. State the context in which geminate consonants degeminate.

181

Ewe Tone

Basic Facts. In the Aŋlɔ dialect of Ewe, syllables can bear the following tones phonetically, among others:

$$á = high (H)$$

$$ā = mid (M)$$

$$à = low (L)$$

In underlying representation, only two distinct tones need be postulated: H and M. Each syllable of a word is underlyingly tone-marked. The tonal processes giving rise to L tones are governed by regular principles.

1. In the following nouns the prefix vowels *a-* and *e-* show tonal alternations between M and L. The first tone of the stem in all cases is H. On what basis can the L tone of the prefix be predicted? State the rule involved.

1.	ēyí	'cutlass'	12.	èkpé	'stone'
2.	àblá	(woman's name)	13.	àgbádzέ	'reed seive'
3.	èxá	'broom'	14.	àtágbó	'thigh'
4.	àgóɖò	'kola nut'	15.	ēmú	'mosquito'
5.	āɲígbá	'floor'	16.	àtʃí	'tree'
6.	ālḗ	'sheep'	17.	ēŋɔ́	'worm'
7.	àdzó	(woman's name)	18.	ēmɔgã̂	'fort'
8.	àʃíkέ	'tail'	19.	àtɔtɔ́	'pineapple'
9.	ètó	'ear'	20.	àɸétɔ́	'master'
10.	ēnú	'thing'	21.	èsɔtsú	'stallion'
11.	ēwɔ́	'flour'	22.	āɲákó	(place name)

2. Some further nouns are illustrated in the following data. Here the first stem tone is non-high (M or L) in all cases. Notice that some nouns vary in tone according to whether they are spoken in isolation or before the article *lá*. (The nouns in 1 do not show this alternation.) State in clear prose the rules necessary to account for these forms. One rule should account for L tones in stems and another for L tones in prefixes.

23.	àgbà	'load'	àgbà lá	'the load'
24.	èdà	'bow'	èdà lá	'the bow'
25.	èlã̀	'animal'	ēlã̄ lá	'the animal'
26.	àkplò	'bag'	ākplō lá	'the bag'
27.	àgò	'velvet'	àgò lá	'the velvet'
28.	ètè	'yam'	ētē lá	'the yam'
29.	èɲì	'cow'	ēɲī lá	'the cow'
30.	èkè	'root'	ēkē lá	'the root'

31.	ègè	'beard'	ègè lá	'the beard'
32.	àyɛ̀	'trick'	āyɛ̄ lá	'the trick'
33.	àsrã̀	'malaria'	āsrã̄ lá	'the malaria'
34.	èɖà	'hair'	èɖà lá	'the hair'
35.	èdzè	'salt'	èdzè lá	'the salt'
36.	èɸè	'year'	ēɸē lá	'the year'
37.	èwɔ̀	'white hair'	ēwɔ̄ lá	'the white hair'
38.	èβè	'hole'	èβè lá	'the hole'
39.	àgbèlì	'cassava'	àgbèlì lá	'the cassava'
40.	àdzàlɛ̀	'soap'	àdzàlɛ̀ lá	'the soap'

3. Formulate the simplest set of rules required to account for tone in Ewe nouns. Your rules should account for all the data in sections 1 and 2, and should have no exceptions. Show specifically how these rules account for the L tones in 'broom', 'bag', and 'the load'.

Kikuyu Verb Conjugation

The following forms illustrate two verb tenses in Kikuyu. Tones are indicated as follows:

$$á = \text{high}$$

$$a = \text{low (unmarked)}$$

A.	Current imperfect.	'look at'	'send'
1.	'we are V-ing'	torɔraɣa	totomáɣa
2.	'we are V-ing him/her'	tomorɔraɣa	tomotomáɣa
3.	'we are V-ing them'	tomarɔ́raɣa	tomatómáɣa
4.	'they are V-ing'	márɔraɣa	mátómáɣa
5.	'they are V-ing him/her'	mámórɔraɣa	mámótomáɣa
6.	'they are V-ing them'	mámárɔ́raɣa	mámátómáɣa

B.	Current past.		
7.	'we V-ed'	torɔrirέ	totomírέ
8.	'we V-ed him/her'	tomorɔrirέ	tomotomírέ
9.	'we V-ed them'	tomarɔ́rirέ	tomatómírέ
10.	'they V-ed'	márɔ́rirέ	mátómírέ
11.	'they V-ed him/her'	mámórɔrirέ	mámótomírέ
12.	'they V-ed them'	mámárɔ́rirέ	mámátómírέ

1. Identify the following morphemes, ignoring the tone.

   'look at'

   'send'

   '1st plural subject'

   '3rd plural subject'

   '3rd singular object'

   '3rd plural object'

   'current imperfect'

   'current past'

2. Now consider the tone. The simplest way of describing these verbs is to assume that each morpheme has a fixed basic tone (high or low). A simple phonological rule will describe all the surface tones. State the rule. (Hint: this rule has no segmental conditioning.) Enter the basic tones to the right of each morpheme identified in 1.

Stress in Selkup (Ostyak-Samoyed)

State the principle of stress distribution illustrated in the words below in ordinary English. Then formulate the rule in terms of metrical trees.

1.	kə̀	'winter'	15.	sɔ́rɨ	'white'
2.	kɨpɔ́:	'tiny'	16.	qó:kɨtɨlʸ	'deaf'
3.	ámɨrna	'eats'	17.	kanaŋmɨ́:	'our dog'
4.	qólʸcɨmpatɨ	'found'	18.	ilɨsɔ́:mɨt	'we lived'
5.	pünakɨsɔ́:	'giant!'	19.	sǽ:qɨ	'black'
6.	úŋŋɨntɨ	'wolverine'	20.	kárman	'pocket'
7.	qúmmɨn	'human being' (gen.)	21.	ú:cɨqo	'to work'
8.	qúmɨm	'human being' (acc.)	22.	ú:cak	'I work'
9.	qúmɨnɨk	'human being' (dat.)	23.	u:cɔ́:mɨt	'we work'
10.	qumó:qɪ	'two human beings'	24.	ú:cɨkkak	'I am working'
11.	qúmɨt	'human beings'	25.	u:cɨkkó:qɪ	'they two are working'
12.	qúmmɨ	'my friend'	26.	ú:cɨtɨlʸ	'working' (part.)
13.	qummɨ́:	'our friend'	27.	ú:cɨlæ	'working' (gerund)
14.	qumo:qlɪlɪ́:	'your two friends'			

Stress in Piro

In Piro phrases, stress is distributed as follows:

1. Primary stress falls on the penultimate syllable.
2. Secondary stress falls on the initial syllable.
3. Tertiary stress falls on every other syllable following the secondary stress, except that in phrases with an odd number of syllables the syllable preceding the one with primary stress is stressless, and there is never any stress on the last syllable.

Give a formal statement in metrical terms of the Piro stress rule.

Sources

Chapter 2

Angas: D. A. Burquest, "A Preliminary Study of Angas Phonology", *Studies in Nigerian Languages* 1, Institute of Linguistics, Zaria (Nigeria), 1971.

Kongo: L. I. Ferraz, (see São Tomé Creole)

Ewe: G. N. Clements

Ganda: G. N. Clements

Papago: K. L. Hale, "Some Preliminary Observations on Papago Morphophonemics", *IJAL* 31, 295—305, 1965.

Proto-Bantu: J. H. Greenberg, "The Tonal System of Proto-Bantu", *Word* 4.3, 196—208, 1948.

Lowland Murut: D. J. Prentice, *The Murut Languages of Sabah.* Australian National University, Pacific Linguistics Series C, No. 18, 1971.

Mohawk: Nancy Bonvillain, *A Grammar of Akwesasne Mohawk.* National Museum of Man, Canada.

Squamish: Vicky Bergvall, based on data from A. H. Kuipers, *The Squamish Language*, Mouton and Co., The Hague, 1967.

Thai: Richard B. Noss, *Thai Reference Grammar*, Foreign Service Institute, Washington, D.C., 1964.

Chapter 3

Cambodian: Franklin E. Huffman, "The Boundary between the Monosyllable and the Disyllable in Cambodian", *Lingua* 29, 54—66, 1972, and personal communication.

Turkish: Engin Sezer

Welsh: Gwenllian Awberg, "Welsh Mutations: Syntax or Phonology?" *Arch. L.* 6, 14-25, 1975.

Sanskrit: Morris Halle and G. N. Clements

Chapter 4

Turkish: Engin Sezer

Tibetan: Olle Kjellin, "How to Explain the 'Tones' in Tibetan", *Ann. Bull. of the Res. Inst. of Logopedics and Phoniatrics* 9, Tokyo, 1975.

Kikuyu: G. N. Clements

Russian: Morris Halle

Chapter 5

Klamath: M. A. R. Barker, *Klamath Dictionary*, University of California Press, 1963.

Russian: Morris Halle

A Children's Language: J. R. Applegate, "Phonological Rules of a Subdialect of English", *Word* 17, 186—193, 1961.

Mohawk: Paul Postal, *Aspects of Phonological Theory*, Harper and Row, New York, 1968 and "Mohawk Vowel Doubling", *IJAL* 35, 291—298, 1969.

Indonesian: G. N. Clements

Japanese: S. Kuno and W. Poser

German: R. E. Keller, *German Dialects*, Manchester University Press, 1961.

Kirghiz: C. D. Johnson, "Regular Disharmony in Kirghiz," in Robert M. Vago, ed., *Issues in Vowel Harmony*, John Benjamins B.V., Amsterdam, 1980.

Bamileke: L. M. Hyman, *A Phonological Study of Fe?fe?-Bamileke*, Studies in African Linguistics, Supplement 4, 1972.

Swahili: G. N. Clements

Turkish: E. Sezer

São Tomé Creole: L. I. Ferraz, "The Creole of São Tomé", *African Studies* 37.1, 3—68 and 37.2, 235—288, 1978.

Klamath: M. A. R. Barker. *Klamath Dictionary*, University of California Press, 1963.

Russian: Morris Halle

Another Children's Language: N. V. Smith, *The Acquisition of Phonology*, Cambridge University Press, Cambridge, 1973.

Yokuts: S. Y. Kuroda, *Yawelmani Phonology*, M.I.T. Press, 1967.

Latvian: Morris Halle

Okpe: Carl Hoffman, "The Vowel Harmony System of the Okpe Monosyllabic Verb", *Research Notes* 6, 1—3, pp. 79—112, University of Ibadan (Nigeria), Department of Linguistics and Nigerian Languages, 1973.

Icelandic: H. Thráinsson

Ancient and Modern Greek: Brian D. Joseph

Chapter 6

Arabic: J. McCarthy, "A Prosodic Account of Arabic Broken Plurals", in I. R. Dihoff, ed., *Current Approaches to African Linguistics*, Foris Publications, 1982.

Ogori: B. S. Chumbow, "Contraction and Tone Polarization in Ogori", *Journal of West African Languages* 12, 89—103, 1982.

Mende: W. Leben, "The Representation of Tone," in V. Fromkin, ed., *Tone: a Linguistic Survey*, Academic Press, New York, 1978.

Southern Paiute: E. Sapir, "La réalité psychologique des phonèmes." *Journal de Psychologie Normale et Pathologique* 30, 247—265, 1933 and K. Hale (personal communication).

Ewe: G. N. Clements

Kikuyu: G. N. Clements

Selkup: A. N. Kuznecova, E. A. Xelimskij, and E. V. Gruškina, *Očerki po sel'kupskomu jazyku*, Izdatel'stvo Moskovskogo Universiteta, Moscow, 1980.

Piro: E. Matteson, *The Piro (Arawakan) Language*, University of California Press, Berkeley and Los Angeles, 1965, and D. Massam (personal communication).

Languages

Chapter 2

Angas:	Chadic, Afro-Asiatic	Nigeria
Kongo:	Bantu	Angola
Ewe:	Niger-Congo	Ghana
Ganda:	Bantu	Uganda
Papago:	Uto-Aztecan	Arizona, Mexico
Proto-Bantu:	Niger-Congo	West Africa
Lowland Murut:	Northwest Austronesian	Borneo
Mohawk:	Iroquoian	Quebec, Ontario, New York
Squamish:	Salish	British Columbia
Thai:	Kam-Tai	Thailand

Chapter 3

English:	Germanic, Indo-European	North America, Great Britain, Australia
Cambodian:	Mon-Khmer	Cambodian
Turkish:	Altaic	Turkey
Welsh:	Celtic, Indo-European	Wales
Sanskrit:	Indic, Indo-European	survives as a liturgical language in India

Chapter 4

Tibetan:	Tibeto-Burman	Tibet, India
Kikuyu:	Bantu	Kenya
Russian:	Slavic, Indo-European	U.S.S.R.

Chapter 5

Klamath:	Penutian	Oregon
Indonesian:	Austronesian	Indonesia
Japanese:	Altaic (?)	Japan
German:	Germanic, Indo-European	Germany
Kirghiz:	Altaic	U.S.S.R.
Bamileke:	Niger-Congo	Cameroon
Swahili:	Bantu	East Africa
São Tomé:	Creole of Niger-Congo and Portuguese origin	São Tomé (Africa)
Yokuts:	Penutian	California
Lithuanian:	Baltic, Indo-European	Lithuania (U.S.S.R.)
Latvian:	Baltic, Indo-European	Latvia (U.S.S.R.)
Icelandic:	Germanic, Indo-European	Iceland

| Okpe: | Niger-Congo | Nigeria |
| Greek: | Indo-European | Greece |

Chapter 6

Arabic:	Semitic	North Africa and Near East
Ogori:	Niger-Congo	Nigeria
Mende:	Niger-Congo	West Africa
Southern Paiute:	Uto-Aztecan	Arizona and Utah
Selkup:	Ostyak-Samoyed	West Siberia (between the Ob and Yenisey rivers)
Piro:	Arawakan	Columbia and Ecuador

PROBLEM BOOK IN PHONOLOGY

Bradford Books

Edward C. T. Walker, Editor. *Explorations in THE BIOLOGY OF LANGUAGE.* The M.I.T. Work Group in the Biology of Language: Noam Chomsky, Salvador Luria, *et alia.* 1979.

Daniel C. Dennett. *BRAINSTORMS: Philosophical Essays on Mind and Psychology.* 1979.

Charles E. Marks. *COMMISSUROTOMY, CONSCIOUSNESS AND UNITY OF MIND.* 1980.

John Haugeland, Editor. *MIND DESIGN.* 1981.

Fred I. Dretske. *KNOWLEDGE AND THE FLOW OF INFORMATION.* 1981.

Jerry A. Fodor. *REPRESENTATIONS: Philosophical Essays on the Foundations of Cognitive Science.* 1981.

Ned Block, Editor. *IMAGERY.* 1981.

Roger N. Shepard and Lynn A. Cooper. *MENTAL IMAGES AND THEIR TRANSFORMATIONS.* 1982.

John Macnamara. *NAMES FOR THINGS: A Study of Human Learning.* 1982.

Hubert L. Dreyfus, Editor, in Collaboration with Harrison Hall. *HUSSERL, INTENTIONALITY AND COGNITIVE SCIENCE.* 1982.

Natalie Abrams and Michael D. Buckner, Editors. *MEDICAL ETHICS: A Clinical Textbook and Reference for the Health Care Professions.* 1983.

Morris Halle and G. N. Clements. *PROBLEM BOOK IN PHONOLOGY: A Workbook for Introductory Courses in Linguistics and in Modern Phonology.* 1983.